Accounting for Derivatives and Hedging Activities

Accounting for Derivatives and Hedging Activities

Frank J. Beil

Accounting for Derivatives and Hedging Activities
Copyright © Business Expert Press, LLC, 2013.

First published in 2013 by
Business Expert Press, LLC
222 East 46th Street, New York, NY 10017
www.businessexpertpress.com

ISBN-13: 978-1-60649-590-2 (paperback)
ISBN-13: 978-1-60649-591-9 (e-book)

Business Expert Press Financial Accounting and Auditing collection

Collection ISSN: 2151-2795 (print)
Collection ISSN: 2151-2817 (electronic)

Cover and interior design by Exeter Premedia Services Private Ltd., Chennai, India

First edition: 2013

10 9 8 7 6 5 4 3 2 1

Printed in the United States of America.

Abstract

Derivatives, and derivatives used to hedge financial and operating functions, are designed to allow managers of firms to manage effectively the downside risk of their financial and operating strategies. They also can be very useful tools that allow managers and executives to accurately predict financial and operational performance and manage the investment communities' "expectations" regarding overall firm performance.

Derivatives and hedges, however, if not properly designed in conjunction with the firm's risk management strategy, can be potentially disastrous for the firm. The ongoing financial turmoil in markets can be partially explained by company managers and executives not understanding the potential financial statement impact when derivative markets move in a particular direction for longer periods of time than anticipated by firms.

This book is designed for managers and executives to be a comprehensive yet accessible resource for understanding the impact of derivative and hedge accounting on a company's reporting of financial statements. The book's primary purpose is to demystify derivatives and provide practical advice and counsel on how to use them to manage more effectively the operational and financial risks to the firm. When used properly, derivatives are an extremely effective tool that managers and executives can use to reduce uncertainty regarding the future.

Keywords

derivatives, hedges, hedging, financial instruments, foreign currency, hedge effectiveness, cash flows, fair value, forwards, options, futures, swaps, interest rate derivatives

Contents

Examples Index

CHAPTER 1

Financial Reporting Implications

About This Chapter

Derivative instruments are very useful risk management tools that can be used by companies to effectively manage the financial and operating risks that all firms face in uncertain business environments. The deployment of these financial instruments, when used properly, will allow managers to more accurately predict their financial and operating performance and better manage the investment communities "expectations" regarding overall firm performance. Derivative instruments are very effective at hedging price or market risk, interest rate risk, and foreign exchange risk.

Our focus in this chapter is to gain an understanding of the accounting implications on the company's financial statements when using derivatives as hedging instruments as part of the company's risk management strategy. Throughout this chapter and the remaining chapters, we will focus on managing the following risks: market price movements, interest rate movements, foreign exchange movements, and credit quality. By gaining a clear perspective of which risk we are managing (price, interest rate, foreign exchange, credit), we will be better able to use derivatives to hedge away a major share of our potential downside risk.

This book is written from the standpoint of operating and financial managers using derivatives as part of an overall risk management strategy. The book is not about using derivatives for speculative purposes as part of an investment strategy. It is designed to be a practical guide to the tools and techniques companies use as part of an overall risk management strategy.

Accounting Mechanics

Accounting guidance for derivatives follows three fundamental principles.

1. Derivative instruments represent rights (assets) or obligations (liabilities) that meet the definitions of assets—expected future cash inflows or liabilities—expected future cash outflows and these assets and liabilities are reported in the financial statements.
2. Fair value is the most relevant measure for financial instruments and the only relevant measure of derivative instruments.
3. Special accounting for items designated as being hedged is provided only for qualifying transactions. The most important criterion for qualification for the special accounting treatment for hedging transactions is for the derivative instrument to be highly effective in offsetting fair value changes in the hedged item.

One of the complexities in recognizing a derivative instruments impact on the financial statements is in identifying what constitutes a derivative in accounting guidance. The accounting standard setter's definition of a derivative instrument essentially says that almost any financial transaction could be considered a derivative. Their definition of a derivative is any financial instrument that contains the following characteristics.[1]

1. The contract contains an underlying variable, interest rate index, commodity price, exchange rate, or any other variable, including the occurrence or nonoccurrence of a specified event. *If the occurrence or nonoccurrence of a specified event causes variability in the cash flows to either party to the contract, then under this criterion we would potentially have a derivative.* The contract contains a notional amount or a payment provision, or both, such as the fixed number of currency units, shares, pounds, or any other unit specified in the contract. The interaction between the *underlying variable and the notional amount* determines the amount of settlement, and in some cases whether or not settlement is required.
2. The contract contains *no initial net investment or an initial net investment that is smaller* than would be required of other types of contracts

that would be expected to have a similar response to changes in market factors. For example, an option to purchase a share of common stock is valued at far less than purchasing the share at market price.

3. The contract *requires or permits net settlement*, and can be readily settled net by means outside the contract, for example trade out of the option above prior to purchasing the underlying shares. Or, the contract provides for delivery of an asset that puts the recipient in a position not substantially different from net settlement, that is, taking delivery of a commodity as a result of a futures contract or being able to net settle the derivative instrument for cash.

The definition of a derivative instrument above needs to be applied to every financial or commodity contract that the company enters into in order to determine if the contract contains any embedded or freestanding derivatives. (Appendix II covers embedded derivatives, the chapters deal with what in accounting are called freestanding derivatives.) This lack of clarity from the standard setters in their definition of what types of financial instruments constitute a derivative instrument makes even identifying whether or not you have a derivative difficult. In my view, the two most important considerations in determining the presence of a derivative in a financial contract are: (a) is there a mechanism contained in the terms and conditions of the contract by which the cash flows could vary on either side of the contract, and (b) are the cash flows to be paid/received determined by multiplying the contractual mechanism that changes the amount to be paid times the notional? (In Appendix I, we will be delving much deeper into the types of financial contracts that require derivative accounting and those contracts that are scoped out of the accounting guidance.)

The following contracts will be used to illustrate the three-step process above that companies need to apply in making the determination as to whether or not their financial contracts constitute a freestanding derivative contract. The chart also serves as an introduction to common derivative instruments that companies use to hedge financial or operational risks.

Contract	Underlying and notional component	No or smaller initial net investment	Permits/requires net settlement	Derivative contract?
Interest rate swap	Payment amount is based on the difference between the contractual rate and the current rate X notional amount for both the company and the counterparty	No amounts are exchanged that relate to the principal (notional) amount	The amount paid to either party to the contract is the difference between the amounts owed or due	Yes
Forward contract to buy or sell an agricultural product (bushels of wheat)	Value of the contract depends on the change in price X quantity (notional).	Since the underlying price at inception of the contract has not changed there would be no initial investment.	It depends on whether or not the agricultural commodity is a traded product. If that is the case then, yes it would be readily convertible to cash. If the commodity is not traded and there is no way to net settle the contract, it would not be readily convertible to cash.	Yes, if a traded commodity and no if it could not be net settled because of a lack of a market mechanism that could potentially turn the commodity into cash.
Futures contract to purchase a commodity	Payment amount based on the difference between the contract price and the current price of the commodity X the notional contractual amount	The margin requirement for futures is collateral not an investment in the contract	Since futures markets are only traded on exchanges, even if physical delivery is made the company would have the option to net settle.	Yes
Foreign currency swap	Payment is based on the difference between the stated exchange rate and the current exchange rate X the notional amount for each party to the contract	Even when the parties to the contract exchange their respective currencies upfront, the net amount is the difference between the assets exchanged, not the notional amount.	The underlying currencies would normally be readily convertible to cash. If one of the currencies is not exchangeable, then this condition not met.	Generally yes
Option on a public company stock	Contract value is the difference between the price stated in the contract (exercise price) and the market price X number of shares (notional).	Even if the option when purchased is in the money it would offer a much larger potential return. (Smaller than purchasing the underlying equity securities.	Even if contractual would require settlement in shares, since publicly traded be readily convertible to cash	Yes

Common Types of Derivative Instruments

Accounting for derivatives guidance is one of the most complex accounting standards ever written by the Financial Accounting Standards Board (FASB). There are literally thousands of possible derivative instruments and hedging strategies that companies could employ to manage their financial and operating risk. (Risk is being defined as "the probability of an uncertain outcome.") Investment banks and commercial banks are in the business of responding to their client needs to manage operating and financial risks. Since most firms have unique needs in managing their business and financial risks, banks will tailor a risk-management strategy around a company's specific needs. This translates to new derivatives being "invented" almost every day. For our purposes, in order for your companies to better understand the economic impact of derivative instruments and its related hedge accounting on the financial statements, this book will concentrate on the most common types of derivative instruments used in practice by companies. The four derivative transactions that are most useful to companies in deploying their risk management strategies are:

- Swaps, including
  - Interest rate swaps
  - Foreign exchange swaps
  - Pricing interest rate swaps
- Forward Contracts
- Futures Contracts
- Option Contracts

These contracts will be explained in the following sections and examples will be used to illustrate the mathematical mechanics of each of these contractual arrangements.

Swaps

A swap is a contractual agreement in which two parties agree to swap (exchange) a series of cash flows at prearranged intervals for a specified period of time. The payments to be paid or received are calculated by applying an agreed-upon formula (normally a benchmark interest rate) on an agreed-upon principal amount. Because the principal is used only to greed-upon cash flows to be transferred between the parties, amount for derivative contracts is called the notional. Swaps ed to exchange between the parties to the contract the cash ιιows ς----- ed by the existing financial contracts. Given the broad definition of a swap, any financial contract with cash flows attached can be swapped. The only requirement is that each party to the contract feels they are better off when engaging in the swap than they would be by not entering into a swap transaction. The movement of the underlying benchmark interest (in the United States there are only two benchmark interest rates: the London Interbank Offer Rate (LIBOR) or the prime rate for credit-worthy customer rate over the term of the swap when multiplied times the notional (principal) amount agreed to by each party to the swap agreement will place one party in a net pay position and the other parties in a net receive position for the contractual cash flows depending upon the movement of the benchmark interest rate (Recently, accounting guidance was changed to allow companies to use the Federal Forward Funds Rate instead of LIBOR.). To simplify accounting, the only cash transferred to either party in a swap is the amount of the net pay computed for each reporting period of the swap. (Accounting guidance requires a derivative instrument be marked to market every three months or on each financial reporting date.)

An *interest rate swap* is a contractual agreement between parties in which each party agrees to make periodic interest payments to the other party for the term of the derivative arrangement. The payments by each party to the contract are determined by the agreed-upon notional and an agreed-upon interest rate, based on a benchmark rate. To facilitate interest rate swaps between parties, the benchmark rate is usually adjusted adding percentage points of interest to the benchmark rate.

The most common type of interest rate swap is when the company has fixed rate debt in the balance sheet (fixed rate payments of interest) and wishes to exchange it for variable (floating) rate debt payments. In this case, the company pays fixed rate interest payments and receives variable rate interest payments from the counterparty. This swap is called a "plain vanilla" interest rate swap. The swap of interest payments will alter the amounts appearing on the financial statements for each party to the derivative arrangement due to the movement of the variable rate debt payments. To simplify the payments between the parties, only the net payment is made to the party that owes the other party after netting out fixed rate payments and variable rate payments. On a pay fixed, receive variable swap arrangement, if the variable rate is greater than the fixed rate for the reporting period under measurement, then the receive variable would get the net amount of variable rate times the notional over the fixed rate paid.

Manufacturers and retailers can typically access variable rate debt markets more cheaply than accessing fixed income markets. However, their financing needs would generally demand fixed rate funding, because that is what financial institutions prefer. On the other hand, financial institutions may prefer variable rate funding and have access to low-cost fixed rate funds. By combining each party's relative advantage, each party to an interest rate swap can accomplish its objective to have access to funds at a lower rate than either could achieve on its own.

Interest rate swaps are the most common swaps used by companies to manage their risk exposure to changing interest rates. The primary issue to resolve when contemplating this type of swap is that the future variable interest rates are unknown at the time of the swap. However, participants in swaps markets possess a wealth of information, both historical and forward looking for "benchmark" interest rates such as LIBOR and the U.S. prime rate set by large money center banks that cover a wide range of maturities. In the United States as well as in Europe and Asia, there are deep and liquid markets for government and corporate bonds that are rated based on their risk characteristics (generally based on their ability to pay the debt when due).

Note: Accounting standards setters on July 17, 2013, approved use of the Overnight Index Swap (OIS) in valuing interest rate derivatives in addition to LIBOR and the Prime rate as benchmark interest rates. The OIS is called the Federal Funds Effective Swap Rate (FFESR).

Armed with this information a company can construct a "forward yield curve" representing the relationship between the debts yield to maturity (YTM) and the time to maturity. The predicted cash flows of interest can then be discounted in order to determine the Net Present Value (NPV) of the cash flows paid or to be received. At the inception of the swap, the present values of the fixed payments and the present value of the variable payments will net out to zero because the underlying variable interest rates for the transaction have not changed. Over the term of the swap, changes in variable interest rates will cause one party to the swap to be a net payer or a net receiver of cash.

The following example illustrates the mathematics and the economics used for *valuing an interest rate swap*. Company borrows $10,000,000 from a commercial bank. The debt is a three-year variable rate loan with interest paid every six months based on LIBOR plus 1% (100 basis points). The company was concerned with carrying variable rate debt because they expected interest rates to rise. Commercial bank then proposed a swap that would commit the company to pay a fixed interest of 9.75% on the notional principle of $10,000,000. In return, the company would receive a payment of LIBOR plus 1% on the same notional amount in order to pay its variable rate debt on the variable rate debt from the bank. The following analysis is a valuation of the interest rate swap from the perspective of the company. The company is trying to determine if they are "better off" by entering into the swap transaction.[2]

For the variable rate loan the forecasted costs are:

Variable Rate Loan Payments

Time	Forecasted LIBOR (%)	Forecasted variable rate to be paid (%)	Forecasted payments ($)
Inception	8.00	9.00	450,000
6 months	8.50	9.50	475,000
12 months	9.00	10.00	500,000
18 months	9.25	10.25	512,500
24 months	9.40	10.40	520,000
30 months	8.50	9.50	475,000

Note: Forecasted LIBOR (derived from a yield curve supplied by commercial bank) plus the agreed-upon additional 1% will equal the forecasted variable rate to be paid. The forecasted payments column is the notional amount of $10,000,000 times forecasted variable rate to be paid divided by 2 (semiannual interest payments).

For the fixed rate payment on the swap to counterparty the calculation is $10,000,000 × 9.75%/2 = $487,500. This amount will be the same at every semiannual "payment" date.

Economic Value for Company to Enter the Swap

In the table, parentheses means the forecasted payments made to commercial bank for the original debt are less than the fixed rate payments that the company is theoretically making for the swap. (Only the net amount would be paid to commercial bank or received from the bank for the swap agreement.)

Also, the present value calculation is: net cash flows/1.075^t.

Net Present Value of an Interest Rate Swap

Time	Net cash flows ($)	Discount rate (%)	Present value of cash flows ($)
Today	(37,500)	9.75	(37,500)
6 months	(12,500)	9.75	(11,931.85)
12 months	12,500	9.75	11,389.52
18 months	25,000	9.75	21,743.69
24 months	32,500	9.75	26,982.01
30 months	(12,500)	9.75	(9,906.01)
Total		9.75	**777.36**

Since the swap value to the company has a positive net present value, the company should enter into the swap.

Foreign exchange swaps allow companies to better manage foreign currency exchange risk. (Risk of the U.S. dollar strengthening or weakening against the foreign-currency-denominated transaction.) For these types of derivative instruments the main consideration is the exchange rate at which the currencies will be swapped when entering into the swap and at the settlement date of the swap. For example, a U.S. company has just signed a contract with a French company to supply machinery. The U.S. company needs to purchase some additional inputs in France in order to complete the machinery before shipping to your customer. The contractual terms of the arrangement are that your company will not be receiving payment from the French company for 90 days after delivery. Your situation is that you need euros now, but won't be paid in euros for 90 days. A foreign exchange swap can be set up so that you borrow euros now and pay them back in 90 days. The payments would be based on a known currency swap rate, say dollars to euros, and a known notional amount (amount needed to purchase the additional inputs).

Forward Contracts

Forward contracts are arrangements between a buyer and seller (parties to the contract) for delivery of a specified amount of a specific asset at a specified future date. The party that is obligated to take delivery of the specific asset (normally a commodity) takes the *long* position; the party that sells the commodity asset is said to take the *short* position. The separation of the trade date and the delivery date allows the parties to the contract to agree on quantities to be delivered and most importantly the forward price. Instead of settling the contract at the spot price as of the date of delivery of the commodity, the buyer (long position) locks in the price of the asset. This has the effect of changing a variable price to a fixed price for the buyer. Forward contracts are essentially customized futures contracts. The next section contains detailed information on how futures markets work and in particular the pricing mechanisms used to value standardized commodity assets. The principal difference between a forward contract and a futures contract is that futures contracts are almost always swapped and the buyer (long position) does not take delivery of the commodity asset. In forward contracts, the buyer almost always takes delivery of the commodity asset.

Futures Contracts

Futures contracts are actively traded on regulated exchanges in order to produce a more accurate pricing mechanism for the commodity asset. The contracts are standardized as to quantity and price. Their primary purpose is to accommodate buyers and sellers who wish to lock in prices they will pay or sell (receive) for a commodity asset. For example, a cereal company has needs for 10,000,000 (notional amount) bushels of wheat to produce its product. The company is fearful about rising prices and wishes to lock in the price per bushel now for delivery in 90 days. The company then purchases 10,000,000 bushels of wheat at the forward (future) price for delivery in 90 days. Since this derivative transaction is done on an exchange the company has to establish a margin account equal to 5% (percentages may vary) of the notional times the future price. The margin account on the exchange will record, on a daily basis, the status of the value of the futures contract. If the value decreases by greater than 5%, the party in the long position would be required to advance cash funds to insure exchange liquidity. The margin account is closed out by the exchange on settlement date and each party then, depending on their position, pays or receives cash.

Option Contracts

An option contract gives its owner the right, but not the obligation, to trade assets according to its contractual terms. Financial options are a financial contract with a seller (called the writer of the option) and a buyer (called the option holder). The seller has the right to receive an upfront cash payment from the buyer. In return for cash paid, the option holder has the right to require the writer of the option to perform under the contract. The cash received by the writer from the holder is compensation for any obligations the holder may be required to perform.

An option can be either a *call* option or a *put* option. A call option gives the buyer the right to purchase an asset from the writer of the option at a specified price over a specified period of time. If the price movements are not favorable for the holder of the option, then they would let the option expire. A put option gives the holder of the option the right to sell an asset to the writer of the option at a specified price over a specified period of time. There are also differences between American options and European options. American options can be exercised at any time by the holder over the specified term. European options are exercised on the last day of the period of time specified in the contract.

The valuation of options is based on the Black Sholes Merton (BSM) model. Any Excel-based software will allow you to determine the value of a written option as of the date the option is written. Briefly, a call or put option is in the money when the underlying asset that can be bought (call) or sold (put) is greater than the original price of the option. The option holder, theoretically, has no limit to the upside, and is protected on the downside by the cost of purchasing the written option.

Option values are determined using a mathematical formula (Excel-based software produces a value after you input the variables). The valuation of the option is based on the interplay between the following variables.

Exercise (strike) price: Price at which the holder of the option can acquire the underlying asset (for American options, exercise at any time over the life of the option contract, and for European options, at the end of the contractual term).

Current stock price: Value of a call or put option will depend on the market price of the underlying asset when the option is written.

Maturity: The longer the contractual term of the option, the more likely there could be large swings (in the money or out of the money) in the value of the underlying asset

Interest rates: Options are valued generally at the risk-free rate over the term of the contractual agreement with the holder

Volatility: This is the most important factor in determining option valuation. This variable is a measure of how likely the underlying asset will move in or out of money. The determination of option value depends largely on a statistical measure (volatility) of how much the price of the underlying asset can change in one year. For example, let's assume the underlying asset value is $40 and the asset has experienced volatility of 30% for over the previous 12 months. (Volatility is usually calculated over a 12-month period) Mathematically, this means that the underlying asset price has a 67% chance of fluctuating in price from $52 to $38. (Calculation is just taking the $40 × 30% and adding or subtracting the $12 to the $40). The BSM model then takes this mathematical change in the price for each trading day over the number of days contained in the options contract. It is the principal driver of option valuation.

Hedge Accounting

Hedge accounting is a special accounting treatment for the hedged item, existing asset or liability, firm commitment or expected future cash inflows or outflows, and the derivative instrument (forward contracts, interest rate swaps, etc.). Qualifying for the hedge designation allows the company to manage its risk exposure by using changes in the fair value of the hedged item that will likely offset the fair value adjustment (mark-to-market accounting) that is required on the derivative instrument. The accounting impact is to record the increase/decrease in the fair value of the hedged item, which is offset by recording the increase/decrease in the derivative instrument in the same reporting period.

The result of attaching a derivative to the hedged item is that companies that are actively managing their risk exposures may find it useful that the derivative instrument's and the hedged item's changes in fair value are both reflected in the financial statements in the same period under measurement for reporting financial statement results. Because this accounting treatment defers recognition of gains and losses on derivatives, there are numerous restrictions at inception of the hedge and over the life of the hedge in order for companies to qualify for this desired accounting treatment. These criteria will receive detailed attention in Chapter 2 "Hedge Criteria and Effectiveness."

Accounting guidance allows for three types of hedges to be used in a managing price (market) risk, interest rate risk, and foreign exchange risk. The hedge types are:

Fair Value Hedges are hedges of an existing asset, liability, or firm commitment. The fair value hedge is a hedge of an exposure to changes in fair value of a particular risk of the hedged item. For example, to hedge price (market) risk related to a commodity, a company may use futures contracts to lock in the price. The effect of entering into a futures contract for the commodity is to transform the fixed cash flows expected from the asset, liability, or firm commitment into variable cash flows. A firm commitment can be defined as follows.[3]

An agreement with an unrelated party, binding on both parties and usually legally enforceable, with the following characteristics:

a. The agreement specifies all significant terms, including the quantity to be exchanged, the fixed price, and the timing of the transaction. The fixed price may be expressed as a specified amount of an entity's functional currency or of a foreign currency. It may also be expressed as a specified interest rate or specified effective yield. The binding provisions of an agreement are regarded to include those legal rights and obligations codified in the laws to which such an agreement is subject. A price that varies with the market price of the item that is the subject of the firm commitment cannot qualify as a fixed price. For example, a price that is specified in terms of ounces of gold would not be a fixed price if the market price of the item to be purchased or sold under the firm commitment varied with the price of gold.

b. The agreement includes a disincentive for nonperformance that is sufficiently large to make performance probable. In the legal jurisdiction that governs the agreement, the existence of statutory rights to pursue remedies for default equivalent to the damages suffered by the no defaulting party, in and of itself, represents a sufficiently large disincentive for nonperformance to make performance probable for purposes of applying the definition of a firm commitment.

Fair value hedges will be discussed extensively in Chapter 2 "Hedge Criteria and Hedge Effectiveness," Chapter 3 "Accounting for Fair Value Hedges," and Chapter 5 "Accounting for Foreign Currency Hedges."

Cash Flow Hedges are hedges of the company's exposure to the variability in expected future cash flows of recognized assets, liabilities, or unrecognized forecasted transactions. Cash flow hedges fix the price (amount) of what would normally be variable expected cash flows. Cash flow hedges are used to hedge forecasted transactions. Forecasted transactions are defined as

a transaction that is expected to occur for which there is no firm commitment. Because no transaction or event has yet occurred and the transaction or event when it occurs will be at the prevailing market price, a forecasted transaction does not give an entity any present rights to future benefits or a present obligation for future sacrifices.[4]

Cash flow hedges will be discussed extensively in Chapter 2, Chapter 4, and Chapter 5.

Hedges of net investments in foreign subsidiaries hedge the translation (when a foreign company's financial statements are combined with the parent company's financial statements) and transaction exposures due to changes in foreign exchange rates. A hedge of the net investment in foreign subsidiaries is essentially a hedge of the change in the foreign company's net assets (assets minus liabilities) due to changes in the foreign currency against the U.S. dollar. This is the only hedge permitted in which the underlying is not an existing asset, liability, firm commitment, or expected cash flows to purchase or sell an asset or incur a liability. Net investment hedges will be discussed extensively in Chapter 5.

Overview: Fair Value Hedge Accounting

A *fair value hedge* is used to turn fixed cash flows into variable cash flows. For example, a company has fixed rate debt and wants to have variable rate exposure for interest expense payments because it believes that interest rates are trending downward. The company would use an interest rate swap and receive variable rate payments from the counterparty. The company has now substituted its fixed payments to the debt holders for variable payments from the counterparty since the variable rate payments are valued by the market at each payment date at their fair value. The company has locked in the amount of debt it would pay without incurring a loss on the debt. (Variable rate debt for each reporting date is reported at fair value.) This is the case because any gain or loss on the debt that needs to be recorded is offset by the derivative (interest rate swap) recording an offsetting gain or loss depending on the movement of interest rates. So, the company has executed a fair value hedge of an existing liability and greatly reduced income statement volatility for its interest payments.

The accounting treatment of a hedged transaction that is designated as a fair value hedge is to use mark-to-market (fair value) accounting for the derivative instrument with recognition of gain or loss in the income statement when the derivative moves in or out of the money. (In the money would be an asset and out of the money would be a liability.) For the hedged item, the accounting treatment is to record changes in fair value from inception of the hedge as gain or loss when the recognized asset, liability, or firm commitment moves in or out of the money. The recognized asset, liability, or firm commitment moves in or out of the money (in the money would represent a gain, while out of the money would represent a liability) when on a reporting date it would cost more to purchase, for example, inventory that has had a price increase, which would result in a loss. This occurs because under derivative accounting the hedged item (inventory) is assumed to be "purchased" on the reporting date. However, the forward contract to purchase inventory would be in the money, and the loss on inventory purchase would be offset by the gain on the derivative instrument. The derivative instrument is in the money because it would allow the company to exercise the derivative and purchase inventory at less than its market price.

To illustrate the accounting and financial statement implications for a fair value hedge, assume the following. The examples used in this chapter are designed to demonstrate the core principles for a fair value and cash flow hedge. When we get the respective chapter for fair value hedges, we will add all the bells and whistles that can complicate accounting for hedging activities. Our purpose in this chapter is to understand the mathematics and financial statement impacts in general of using hedge accounting as part of your overall risk management strategy.

Fair Value Hedge of an Equipment Purchase in Foreign Currency

On, December 1, 20X1, a company enters into a contract with a foreign supplier to purchase equipment (a firm commitment) at a fixed price denominated in a foreign currency, of 200,000 Foreign Currencies (FCs). Management believes the dollar ($) will weaken against the FC and decides to enter into a contract to buy the FC forward contract by matching the delivery date at a fixed price, which will lock in the exchange rate at today's exchange rate. The equipment will be delivered in 90 days and payment is due on delivery. Payment date is February 28, 20X2. The company then locks in the forward rate of FC 1.00 = $0.66.[5]

Additional Information:
Spot rates represent the dollar equivalences that are in effect for that day. That is the price the company would pay to acquire the equipment on that day. The forward rates represent the value of the derivative for the length of time remaining until settlement. The spot and forward rate converge on the settlement date. (Note: Foreign Currency derivatives and hedges will be discussed extensively in Chapter 5.)

Note: Throughout the book, I will use the terms "in the money" and "out of money" for both the derivative instrument (in this case, the forward contract) which is valued using the change in forward rates from December 1, 20X1 to December 31, 20X1 (which is a reporting date) and from December 31, X1 to February 28, 20X2, which is the settlement date and the hedged item. The hedged item (firm commitment) is also valued using the changing forward rates.

In the following table, the derivative instrument (forward contract) on December 31, 20X1, goes in the money because you contracted at inception at FC 1 = $0.66 and you could close out the position at the reporting date at FC 1 = $0.68 resulting in a gain of $4,000. (Notional of FC 200,000 times ($0.68 − $0.66). The offset account of the gain on hedge is the asset account futures contract. The asset account represents that the derivative instrument is in the money.

Now, let's examine the firm commitment. Since we are also valuing the firm commitment to purchase machinery at the forward rate, the mathematics works the same way. Accounting guidance assumes that I hypothetically purchase the machinery on the reporting date and on the settlement date using FC. The math is that we would hypothetically purchase the machinery at FC 200,000 × $0.68 = $136,000 which is $4,000 greater than the forward price on December 31, X1 of FC 200,000 × $0.66 = $132,000. The hypothetical extra cash flow outlay to acquire the asset is recorded as a loss on hedge with the balance sheet offset account a firm commitment liability. The liability account for the hedged item represents the commitment to purchase being out of money.

Spot and Forward Rates for the Forward Contract

Date	Spot rates	Forward rates for 2/28/20X2
December 1, X1	FC 1.00 = $0.65	FC 1.00 = $0.66
December 31, X1	FC 1.00 = $0.66	FC 1.00 = $0.68
February 28, X2	FC 1.00 = $0.69	FC 1:00 = $0.69

Note: $ refers to U.S. dollars

Note: Spot rates and forward rates always converge on settlement date of the hedged transaction.

The following illustrates the financial statement effects.

Assets =	Liabilities +	Stockholder's equity
		+ Gain on hedge – Loss on hedge

December 1, 20X1: Company purchases the 90-day forward contract to hedge its firm commitment to purchase machinery

No value of the forward contract at inception because the underlying variable that values the derivative has not moved (forward price)

December 31, 20X1: Company reports the change in fair value of the derivative instrument and the firm commitment assets =	Liabilities +	Stockholder's equity
+ Forward contract + 4,000		+ Gain on Hedge + 4,000

Assets =	Liabilities +	Shareholder's equity
	+ Firm commitment + 4,000	– Loss on Hedge – 4,000

Note: The computation is $200,000 × (.68 − .66) = $4,000. The fair value comparison is forward to forward rates. The forward contract is recorded as an asset and the firm commitment is recorded as a liability. Together, they offset each other and produce no net effect on reported net income. It is this pairing of the derivative instrument and the hedged item and recording their respective changes in fair value that is distinctive to accounting for derivatives.

The fair value hedge of the firm commitment on December 31, 20X1, is considered out of the money (liability) when compared to the spot exchange price on December 1, 20X1. The derivative instrument is, however, considered in the money (asset). The financial statement affects will net to zero because the gain and loss are offset as well as the recording of an asset and an equal liability.

February 28, 20X1: Record the fair value change of the derivative instrument and the firm commitment and purchase the equipment

Assets =	Liabilities +	Stockholder's equity
+ Forward contract + 2,000		+ Gain on hedge + 2,000

Assets =	Liabilities +	Stockholder's equity
	+ Firm commitment + 2,000	– Loss on hedge – 2,000

To record the fair value of the firm commitment and the forward contract and recognize gain or loss on the hedge. The computation is $200,000 × (.68 − .69) = 2,000$

Assets =	Liabilities +	Stockholder's equity
+ Equipment + 132,000	– Firm commitment – 6,000 Contract liabilities + 138,000	

To record the equipment purchase at the forward price on December 1, X1 for settlement at February 28, X2 at FC 200,000 × $0.66 = $132,000 and to remove the firm commitment liability from the accounts upon settlement and to record the contract liability at FC 200,000 × $.69 = $138,000.

Assets =	Liabilities +	Stockholder's equity
– Forward contract – 6,000 – Cash – 132,000	– Contract liabilities – 138,000	

Assets =	Liabilities +	Stockholder's equity
	– Contract liabilities – 138,000	

To pay the contract liability of 138,000 after writing off the contractual asset of 6,000 and paying cash of 132,000.

Note: The forward contract is in the money by $6,000. We settle the contract and receive the $6,000. The firm commitment is out of the money by $6,000. The company pays the $138,000 to acquire the machinery, but writes-off the liability account (firm commitment) resulting in a recording balance of the equipment of $132,000.

This is an effective illustration in demonstrating how hedge accounting works. The company wanted to purchase equipment without bearing foreign exchange risk. By entering into a forward contract at inception of the contract the company locks in FC 1.00 = $.66 × 200,000 assuring that the equipment is recorded at that amount and the cash paid is equal to that amount.

Overview of Cash Flow Hedges

A *cash flow hedge* is used to turn variable-expected payments into fixed payments. To demonstrate a cash flow hedge, assume the company has a variable rate debt, which exposes the company to interest rate risk if interest rates on the payments rise. The company would use an interest rate swap where the company pays a fixed rate on its interest payments to counterparty and receives variable rate interest payments. The company would be substituting the fixed rate paid to the counterparty for the floating rate required to be paid to debt holders. (Cash flow hedges will be covered extensively in Chapter 4)

A cash flow hedge is a hedge of a forecasted transaction that is likely to occur in the future. Since the forecasted transaction has not occurred, the accounting treatment in the financial statements is different because we are not "attaching" the derivative to a recognized asset, liability, or firm commitment. Instead, we are hedging the amount of cash to be paid or received on the settlement date of the derivative instrument. While the derivative is required to be recorded at fair value, there will be no offsetting entries to other assets, liabilities, or firm commitments to offset the derivative instrument changes in fair value form going in (asset) or out of the money (liability).

The accounting guidance for cash flow hedges, until settlement date, calls for the use of a Shareholder's Equity account called Other Comprehensive Income (OCI) as the offset account for the derivative instrument. This accounting treatment for cash flow hedges has the hypothetical effect of offsetting the asset or liability recording of the derivative instrument with the opposite entry to shareholder's equity using the OCI account. This accounting treatment has the effect of rendering the financial statement effect of the hedge as nearly offsetting on the balance sheet and no effect on the income statement until the hedge is settled by the company.

Cash Flow Hedge by Using a Futures Contract to Hedge a Raw Materials Purchase

For example, a company enters into a 90-day contract, on December 1, 20X1, to purchase raw materials by entering into a futures contract in order to lock in the price of the raw materials at the inception of the hedged transaction. The contract price is $8 per pound and the contract states we will take delivery of 100,000 pounds on February 28, 20X2. The spot price (the price we could purchase the raw materials inventory) is $7.80 on December 31, 20X1, and $8.30 on February 28, 20X2. The financial statement impact would be as follows.

On December 31, 20X1, we would recognize that the derivative instrument is out of the money by ($7.80 – $8.00) × 100,000 = $20,000). The derivative is out of the money because we could purchase the raw materials inventory at a market price that is less than the contract price.

On February 28, 20X2, we would recognize that the derivative instrument is in the money by ($8.30 – $8.00) × 100,000 = $30,000) and purchase the materials at $8 a pound.

The financial statement effects for a cash flow hedge are illustrated below.

Assets =	Liabilities +	Stockholder's equity
		+ OCI – Deferred gain – OCI – Deferred loss

December 31, 20X1: Recognize the derivative at fair value (market price)

Assets =	Liabilities +	Stockholder's equity
	+ Contract liability + 20,000	– OCI – 20,000

Note that the liability amounts and the stockholder's equity amounts offset and net to -0-.

February 28, 20X1: Recognize the derivative at fair value and settle the cash flow hedge.

Assets =	Liabilities +	Stockholder's equity
+ Derivative Asset + 30,000	– Contract liabilities 20,000	+ OCI + 50,000

Note: The change in fair value of the derivative instrument is $8.30 – $8.00, which is the price change December 31, 20X1, and February 28, 20X2. The recording of the now in-the-money derivative asset is at $30,000 in the company's financial statements. However, since the derivative's change in fair value was $50,000 (from a liability of $20,000 to an asset of $30,000 are offset entry to OCI which is $50,000. This has the financial statement effect of reporting the derivative asset at $30,000 with the offset to and a balance of $30,000 in shareholder's equity via the OCI account of $30,000.

Purchase Inventory at the Market (Spot) Price

Assets =	Liabilities +	Stockholder's equity
+ Inventory + 830,000 – Cash – 830,000		

Note: Commodities are normally purchased at the spot price. We purchase the inventory and pay cash.

Receive Cash for Derivative Being in the Money

Assets =	Liabilities +	Stockholder's equity
+ Cash + 30,000 – Derivative asset – 30,000		

Note: We settle the derivative instrument and receive cash from the futures market. Since this was a cash flow hedge, we protect our payment of cash for inventory, by netting out the $830,000 paid for inventory with the $30,000 received from settling the in-the-money derivative instrument. Lock in at $8 per pound, successful.

Remove OCI Account from Stockholders, Equity and Adjust Inventory

Assets =	Liabilities +	Stockholder's equity
– Inventory – 30,000		– OCI – 30,000

Note: The shareholder's equity account remains on the balance sheet until we settle the hedged transaction. Here is where the hedging transactions "hedged item" comes into play. Since the arrangement was done to protect the inventory purchase, we eliminate the OCI balance against the inventory account. Also, note that when the inventory is sold, our recording of cost of goods sold will be $30,000 less than it would be if we did not hedge.

Our objective in this hedge was to lock in the inventory price of $8.00 a pound. The purchase of inventory at the market price of $8.30 per pound was offset by the derivative instrument going in the money by $.30 per pound. We receive the $30,000 cash from settling the contract, which reduces our net cash flow cost of the inventory to $800,000. In addition, we remove the OCI amount of $30,000 on the balance sheet by decreasing inventory to $800,000. Mission accomplished.

Net investment hedges of foreign operations are designed to hedge the company's exposure to foreign exchange risk. For example, financial statements of foreign-owned companies are translated into the reporting currency (U.S.$) as of the reporting date, say fiscal year-end. Since the transactions that comprise the financial statements involve transactions that occurred previously, they would be recorded at the exchange rate that existed when those transactions were settled. The report date exchange will be different than the amounts that were recorded during the year. This exposes the company to exchange rate risk. Companies would hedge the expected differences in exchange rates that occurred on settlement date and exchange rates expected at fiscal year-end, to get a more favorable gain or loss in their stockholders equity.

Accounting Measurements Used for Derivatives

Derivatives are required to be reported at fair value. Accounting guidance defines fair value as "the price that would be received to sell the asset or paid to transfer the liability in an orderly transaction between market participants at the measurement date."[6] Accountants use a hierarchy of market inputs to determine the appropriate fair value measurement to be used to value the derivative.

The fair value hierarchy is as follows:

Level 1: Price × Quantity, unadjusted; market inputs for identical assets or liabilities (since derivative valuation until settlement can fluctuate, this would generally not be an appropriate valuation metric).

Level 2: Price × Quantity, adjusted; market inputs for similar assets and liabilities OR extrapolations of current market activity that is expected to continue in the future. For example, forward and commodity yield curves can be constructed from historical data about price movement or interest rate movements.

Level 3: Unobservable inputs that the company uses to proxy what it believes market participants would use in valuing assets or liabilities. For example, interest rate swaps are not traded on an exchange that would then require that their valuation be a discounted cash flow computation depending on the length of time of the swap and the underlying benchmark interest rate used to value the derivative, with an assumption as to the shape of the yield curve for the benchmark rate (i.e., predicting interest rate changes over the term of the hedged transaction). This valuation technique is generally called mark-to-model accounting.

When valuing derivatives, we generally use a mark-to-model methodology in determining the financial statement effects when accounting for derivative instruments and hedging activities. The accounting guidance for derivatives requires the use of fair value measurements. Application of fair value measurements will be used in the numerous illustrations in the book for fair value, cash flow, and foreign currency hedges. This approach to illustrating mark-to-model accounting (fair value) by using specific hedging strategies to achieve the firms risk management strategy should be highly effective in demonstrating the fair value techniques used in accounting for derivative instruments and hedging activities.

To better illustrate the valuation concepts and demonstrate the accounting for derivatives, we will walk through the computations for an interest rate swap.

Fair Value Measurement for an Interest Rate Swap

On January 1, X1, a Finance Company enters into a 3-year receive-fixed, pay-variable (floating) interest rate swap. The fixed rate is at 7% and the notional is $10,000,000. The variable rate resets annually on 12/31 for the next year's rate. The company has $10,000,000 of debt on the balance sheet that pays $7.5% to debt holders.[7] You are given the following information:

	Rate of upcoming year	Fair value	Change in fair value
01/01/X1	7%	—	—
12/31/X1	6%	180,000	180,000
12/31/X2	5%	190,000	10,000
12/31/X3	—		(190,000)

The fair values given above are calculated as the sum of the present value of expected future cash flows. For example: ($10,000,000 × (7%–6%) × 2) / (1.06^2) = $180,000. Note that we assume at 12/31/X1 when the variable rate resets to 6%, we assume it will stay at that rate for 20X2 and 20X3.

Since we assume in this example that the yield curve is flat meaning the 6% interest rate reset is used to value payments for X2 and X3, we would have a level 3 measurement.

Financial Statement Template

Assets =	Liabilities +	Stockholder's equity
		+ Gain on swap – Loss on swap

1/01/X1—Inception of the Swap

No accounting impact because the interest rate swap agreement is entered into at market value.

12/31/X1—Mark the Swap to Fair Value

Assets =	Liabilities +	Stockholder's equity
+ Interest rate swap + 180,000		+ Gain on swap + 180,000

Fair value the swap at two payments of $100,000 discounted at 6%. The computation is $10,000,000 (notional) × (7%–6%). The swap goes in the money because you are paying in year 2 and expected to pay in year 3, $100,000 less in interest expense payments.

12–31/X1—Cash Receipt of the Swap and Record Interest Expense @ 7.5%

Assets =	Liabilities +	Stockholder's equity
+ Cash + 100,000		+ Interest expense + 100,000

Assets =	Liabilities +	Stockholder's equity
– Cash – 750,000		– Interest expense 750,000

The impact on the financial statements as of the end of the year for Finance is to record the gain on the swap of $180,000 and then record the cash payment received from the counterparty computed as $10,000,000 × (7% – 6% = $100,000, which would be taken against the interest expense recorded as $10,000,000 × 7.5%. (The entry above in Stockholder's Equity is a reduction of the interest expense to be recorded by the company.)

12/31/X2—Fair Value the Swap

Assets =	Liabilities +	Stockholder's equity
+ Interest rate swap + 10,000		+ Gain on swap + 10,000

Fair value the swap based on one remaining payment of $200,000 discounted at 5%. The change in fair value for the swap asset is now $190,000.

12/31/X2—Cash Receipt of the Swap and Record Interest Expense

Assets =	Liabilities +	Stockholder's equity
+ Cash + 200,000		+ Interest expense + 200,000

Assets =	Liabilities +	Stockholder's equity
– Cash – 750,000		– Interest expense 750,000

Payment to be received is $10,000,000 \times (7\% - 5\%) = \$200,000$ from the counterparty to the swap. Note that this has the effect of reducing net interest expense by $200,000 due to the movement in interest rates. Also, note the swap asset is now at $190,000.

12/31/X3—Fair Value the Swap

Assets =	Liabilities +	Stockholder's equity
– Interest rate swap – 190,000		– Loss on swap 190,000

Remove interest rate swap asset from the Finance Company's financial statements. Since we were in the money on our interest payments the company would record a loss on swap to remove the asset from its records.

In this chapter, we have examined the foundational principles of accounting for derivative instruments as well as the valuation of derivatives. The following chapters will first start with exploring hedge effectiveness and doing a deeper dive into fair value, cash flow, and foreign currency hedges.

CHAPTER 2

Hedge Criteria and Effectiveness

About This Chapter

Hedge documentation is necessary at the inception of the hedged transaction to qualify for the favorable accounting treatment allowed by accounting guidance for hedge transactions. The favorable treatment is that the hedging gains and losses from the derivative instrument appear in the income statement at the same time as fair value changes to the hedged item are recorded in the financial statements. It is this symmetry of recording offsetting gains or losses on the derivative instrument with gains or losses from the hedged item (existing asset, liability, firm commitment, or forecasted cash flows that are probable of occurring) that makes hedge accounting attractive as a way to manage the volatility of the company's financial statements.

The documentation requirements are very detailed and if not followed precisely will disqualify the financial transaction from qualifying for special hedge accounting. This chapter will discuss the specific hedging documentation requirements at inception of the hedge and calculating the ongoing effectiveness of the hedge. The chapter will be organized as follows.

- Formal designation and documentation at inception
- Eligibility of hedged items and transactions
- Eligibility of hedging instruments
- Hedge effectiveness

Formal Designation and Documentation at Inception

Hedge documentation for all hedges, fair value, cash flow, or net investment in foreign operations is required at inception to document the following.[1]

- Nature of the hedging relationship, including what is the hedging instrument and what is the hedged item.
- Nature of the risk being hedged—includes market (price) risk, interest rate risk, or foreign currency risk.
- The company's risk management strategy, for example, hedge inventory purchase price increases of a commodity, lock in sales price of commodity, and converting a fixed rate financial instrument to a floating (variable) rate.
- The method that will be used to retrospectively and prospectively assess the hedging instrument's effectiveness in offsetting the exposure to changes in the hedged item's fair value (if a fair value hedge) or hedged transaction's variability in cash flows (if a cash flow hedge) is attributable to the hedged risk. There shall be a reasonable basis for how the entity plans to assess the hedging instrument's effectiveness.
- The method used to measure hedge ineffectiveness.

Additional documentation for a fair value hedge of a firm commitment is a description of a reasonable method for recognizing in earnings the asset or liability representing the gain or loss on the hedged firm commitment. For example, if the firm commitment was for the purchase of equipment, then documentation of how the gain or loss will be depreciated and charged to the income statement over the useful life of the equipment.

Cash flow hedges of a forecasted transaction also require additional documentation.

1. The date on or period within which the forecasted transaction is expected to occur.
2. The specific nature of asset or liability involved (if any).
3. Either of the following:
   a. The expected currency amount for hedges of foreign currency exchange risk, that is, specification of the exact amount of foreign currency being hedged
   b. The quantity of the forecasted transaction for hedges of other risks, that is, specification of the physical quantity—the number

of items or units of measure—encompassed by the hedged fore-casted transaction.

4. The current price of a forecasted transaction shall be identified to satisfy the criterion for offsetting cash flows.

5. The hedged forecasted transaction shall be described with sufficient specificity so that when a transaction occurs, it is clear whether that transaction is or is not the hedged transaction. Thus, a forecasted transaction could be identified as the sale of either the first 15,000 units of a specific product sold during a specified three-month period or the first 5,000 units of a specific product sold in each of the three specific months, but it could not be identified as the sale of the last 15,000 units of that product sold during a three-month period (because the last 15,000 units cannot be identified when they occur, but only when the period has ended).

The following illustrates the formal hedge documentation require-ments for a *fair value hedge of a commodity using a forward contract*.[2]

Jewelry is a manufacturer of gold rings and necklaces. On July 1, 20X1, Jewelry enters into a commitment to purchase 1,000 troy ounces of gold on December 31, 20X1, in New York, at the cur-rent forward rate of $310/troy ounce. Jewelry enters into the com-mitment because its supplier requires a fixed-price contract. However, it would prefer to pay the market price at the time of delivery and record the gold inventory at whatever the market price will be on December 31, 20X1.

Therefore, on July 1, 20X1, Jewelry enters into a six-month forward contract to sell 1,000 troy ounces of gold on December 31, 20X1, in New York, at the current forward rate of $310/troy ounce. Thus, the forward contract essentially unlocks the commit-ment. The forward contract requires net cash settlement on December 31, 20X1, and has a fair value of zero at inception. Jewelry and the derivative counterparty are of comparable creditworthiness and the initial CVA is negligible. Jewelry's formal documentation of the hedging relationship, prepared on the date the hedge is entered into, is as follows:

Table 2.1. Formal Hedge Designation Documentation

Risk management objective and nature of the risk being hedged.	The objective of the hedge is to protect the fair value of the firm commitment from changes in the market price of gold. Changes in the fair value of the forward contract are expected to be—highly effective in offsetting changes in the overall fair value of the entire firm commitment.
Date of designation	July 1, 20X1
Hedging instrument	Forward contract to sell 1,000 troy ounces of gold in New York on December 31, 20X1, for $310/troy ounce.
Hedged item	Firm commitment to buy 1,000 troy ounces of gold in New York on December 31, 20X1, for $310/troy ounce. The firm commitment qualifies for the normal purchase exception.
How hedge effectiveness will be assessed	Hedge effectiveness (both prospective and retrospective) will be assessed based on a comparison of the overall changes in fair value of the forward contract (that is, based on changes in the December 31, 20X1, forward price) and changes in the fair value of the firm commitment to purchase gold (also based on changes in the New York forward price), as expressed by a cumulative dollar-offset ratio. The company will assess effectiveness based on changes in the forward price. At inception, because the critical terms of the forward contract and firm commitment coincide (such as dates, quantities, delivery location, and underlying commodity), the company expects the hedge to be highly effective against changes in the overall fair value of the firm commitment. However, changes in the credit risk of both counterparties in the fair value measurement of the forward contract and of the hedger in the fair value measurement of the firm commitment (the hedged item) will likely cause some ineffectiveness to the hedging relationship that needs to be considered. The hedge meets the criteria for a fair value hedge of a firm commitment.
How hedge ineffectiveness will be measured	Ineffectiveness will be measured on an ongoing basis by comparing the change in the fair value of the firm commitment and the change in the fair value of the forward and any difference will be reflected in earnings as ineffectiveness.

Eligibility of Hedged Items and Transactions

Fair Value Hedges

A company may designate a derivative instrument as hedging the exposure to changes in the *fair value* of an asset or liability (market or price risk) or an identified portion of the asset or liability. An asset or liability is eligible for designation as hedged items in a *fair value hedge* of the following criteria are met.[3]

1. The hedged item is specifically identified as either all or a specific portion of a recognized asset or liability or of an unrecognized firm commitment.
2. The hedged item is a single asset or liability (or a specific portion thereof) or is a portfolio of similar assets or a portfolio of similar liabilities (or a specific portion thereof), in which circumstance:
   a. If similar assets or similar liabilities are aggregated and hedged as a portfolio, the individual assets or individual liabilities shall share the risk exposure for which they are designated as being hedged. The change in fair value attributable to the hedged risk for each individual item in a hedged portfolio shall be expected to respond in a generally proportionate manner to the overall change in fair value of the aggregate portfolio attributable to the hedged risk.
   b. If the hedged item is a specific portion of an asset or liability (or of a portfolio of similar assets or a portfolio of similar liabilities), the hedged item is one of the following:
      i. A percentage of the entire asset or liability (or of the entire portfolio). An entity shall not express the hedged item as multiple percentages of a recognized asset or liability and then retroactively determine the hedged item based on an independent matrix of those multiple percentages and the actual scenario that occurred during the period for which hedge effectiveness is being assessed.
      ii. One or more selected contractual cash flows, including one or more individual interest payments during a selected portion of the term of a debt instrument (such as the portion of the asset or liability representing the present value of the interest payments in the first two years of a four-year debt instrument).
      iii. The residual value in a lessor's net investment in a direct financing or sales-type lease.
3. The hedged item presents an exposure to changes in fair value attributable to the hedged risk that could affect reported earnings. The reference to affecting reported earnings does not apply to an entity that does not report earnings as a separate caption in a statement of financial performance, such as a not-for-profit entity (NFP).

4. If the hedged item is all or a portion of a debt security (or a portfolio of similar debt securities) that is classified as held to maturity in accordance with accounting guidance, the designated risk being hedged is the risk of changes in its fair value attributable to *credit risk or foreign exchange risk*, or both. If the hedged item is an option component of a held-to-maturity security that permits its prepayment, the designated risk being hedged is the risk of changes in the entire fair value of that option component. If the hedged item is other than an option component of a held-to-maturity security that permits its prepayment, the designated hedged risk also shall not be the risk of changes in its overall fair value.

5. If the hedged item is a nonfinancial asset or liability (other than a recognized loan servicing right or a nonfinancial firm commitment with financial components), the designated risk being hedged is the risk of changes in the fair value of the entire hedged asset or liability (reflecting its actual location if a physical asset). That is, the price risk of a similar asset in a different location or of a major ingredient shall not be the hedged risk. Thus, in hedging the exposure to changes in the fair value of gasoline, an entity may not designate the risk of changes in the price of crude oil as the risk being hedged for purposes of determining effectiveness of the fair value hedge of gasoline.

6. If the hedged item is a financial asset or liability, a recognized loan servicing right, or a nonfinancial firm commitment with financial components, the designated risk being hedged is any of the following:

   a. The risk of changes in the overall fair value of the entire hedged item.

   b. The risk of changes in its fair value attributable to changes in the designated benchmark interest rate (referred to as interest rate risk).

   c. The risk of changes in its fair value attributable to changes in the related foreign currency exchange rates (referred to as foreign exchange risk).

   d. The risk of changes in its fair value attributable to both of the following (referred to as credit risk):

    i. Changes in the obligor's creditworthiness.

   ii. Changes in the spread over the benchmark interest rate with respect to the hedged item's credit sector at inception of the hedge.

Cash Flow Hedges

A company may designate a derivative instrument as hedging the exposure to variability in expected future cash flows that is attributable to a particular risk. That exposure may be associated with either of the following:[4]

1. An existing recognized asset or liability (such as all or certain future interest payments on variable-rate debt).
2. A forecasted transaction (such as a forecasted purchase or sale).

A forecasted transaction is eligible for designation as a hedged transaction in a cash flow hedge if all of the following additional criteria are met:

a. The forecasted transaction is specifically identified as either of the following:
    i. A single transaction.
   ii. A group of individual transactions that share the same risk exposure for which they are designated as being hedged. A forecasted purchase and a forecasted sale shall not both be included in the same group of individual transactions that constitute the hedged transaction.
b. The occurrence of the forecasted transaction is probable.
c. The forecasted transaction meets both of the following conditions:
    i. It is a transaction with a party external to the reporting entity.
   ii. It presents an exposure to variations in cash flows for the hedged risk that could affect reported earnings.
d. The forecasted transaction is not the acquisition of an asset or incurrence of a liability that will subsequently be remeasured with changes in fair value attributable to the hedged risk reported currently in earnings.

e. If the forecasted transaction relates to a recognized asset or liability, the asset or liability is not remeasured with changes in fair value attributable to the hedged risk reported currently in earnings.

f. If the variable cash flows of the forecasted transaction relate to a debt security that is classified as held to maturity under Topic 320 : the risk being hedged is the risk of changes in its cash flows attributable to any of the following risks:

   i. Credit risk.

   ii. Foreign exchange risk.

g. The forecasted transaction does not involve a business combination.

h. The forecasted transaction is not a transaction (such as a forecasted purchase, sale, or dividend) involving either of the following:

   i. A parent entity's interests in consolidated subsidiaries.

   ii. An entity's own equity instruments.

i. If the hedged transaction is the forecasted purchase or sale of a nonfinancial asset, the designated risk being hedged is either of the following:

   i. The risk of changes in the functional-currency-equivalent cash flows attributable to changes in the related foreign currency exchange rates.

   ii. The risk of changes in the cash flows relating to all changes in the purchase price or sales price of the asset reflecting its actual location if a physical asset (regardless of whether that price and the related cash flows are stated in the entity's functional currency or a foreign currency), not the risk of changes in the cash flows relating to the purchase or sale of a similar asset in a different location or of a major ingredient. Thus, for example, in hedging the exposure to changes in the cash flows relating to the purchase of its bronze bar inventory, an entity may not designate the risk of changes in the cash flows relating to purchasing the copper component in bronze as the risk being hedged for purposes of assessing offset and hedge effectiveness.

j. If the hedged transaction is the forecasted purchase or sale of a financial asset or liability (or the interest payments on that financial asset or liability) or the variable cash inflow or outflow of an existing financial asset or liability, the designated risk being hedged is any of the following:

i. The risk of overall changes in the hedged cash flows related to the asset or liability, such as those relating to all changes in the purchase price or sales price (regardless of whether that price and the related cash flows are stated in the entity's functional currency or a foreign currency).

ii. The risk of changes in its cash flows attributable to changes in the designated benchmark interest rate (referred to as interest rate risk).

iii. The risk of changes in the functional-currency-equivalent cash flows attributable to changes in the related foreign currency exchange rates (referred to as foreign exchange risk).

iv. The risk of changes in its cash flows attributable to all of the following (referred to as credit risk):

    aa. Default.

    bb. Changes in the obligor's creditworthiness.

    cc. Changes in the spread over the benchmark interest rate with respect to the related financial asset's or liability's credit sector at inception of the hedge.

Qualifying Cash Flow Hedges

A cash flow hedge involves forecasted transactions. In order to qualify, the forecasted transaction has to have a reasonably high level of probability of occurring. The following accounting guidance will assist your company in making the determination if you have achieved the threshold guidance for probable.

1. Effect of counterparty creditworthiness on probability. An entity using a cash flow hedge shall assess the creditworthiness of the counterparty to the hedged forecasted transaction in determining whether the forecasted transaction is probable, particularly if the hedged transaction involves payments pursuant to a contractual obligation of the counterparty.

2. Probability of forecasted acquisition of a marketable security. To qualify for cash flow hedge accounting for an option designated as a hedge of the forecasted acquisition of a marketable security, an entity must be able to establish at the inception of the hedging relationship that the acquisition of the marketable security is probable,

without regard to the means of acquiring it. In documenting the hedging relationship, the entity shall specify the date on or period within which the forecasted acquisition of the security will occur. The evaluation of whether the forecasted acquisition of a marketable security is probable of occurring shall be independent of the terms and nature of the derivative instrument designated as the hedging instrument. Specifically, in determining whether an option designated as a hedge of the forecasted acquisition of a marketable security may qualify for cash flow hedge accounting, the probability of the forecasted transaction being consummated shall be evaluated without consideration of whether the option designated as the hedging instrument has an intrinsic value other than zero.

3. Uncertainty of timing within a range. For forecasted transactions whose timing involves some uncertainty within a range, that range could be documented as the originally specified time period if the hedged forecasted transaction is described with sufficient specificity so that when a transaction occurs, it is clear whether that transaction is or is not the hedged transaction. As long as it remains probable that a forecasted transaction will occur by the end of the originally specified time period, cash flow hedge accounting for that hedging relationship would continue.

4. Importance of timing in both documentation and hedge effectiveness.

5. The term *probable* requires a significantly greater likelihood of occurrence than the phrase *more likely than not*.

6. The cash flow hedging model does not require that it be probable that any variability in the hedged transaction will actually occur—that is, in a cash flow hedge, the variability in future cash flows must be a possibility, but not necessarily a probability. However, the hedging derivative must be highly effective in achieving offsetting cash flows whenever that variability in future interest does occur.

Foreign Currency and Net Investment Hedge

Exposure to a foreign currency exists only in relation to a specific operating unit's designated currency cash flows. Therefore, exposure to foreign currency risk shall be assessed at the unit level. Unit level in this case means a foreign operation that makes its operating and financing decisions based on the local currency in the country or countries in which it operates. If that is the case, then the reporting currency, say U.S.$ is the reporting currency and the local currency is what is called the functional currency. The foreign operating unit then has exposure to foreign currency risk (local currency being converted to reporting currency) ($) if it enters into a transaction (or has an exposure) denominated in the local currency that is different from the company's reported currency ($).

Due to accounting requirement for remeasurement of assets and liabilities denominated in a foreign currency into the unit's reporting currency, changes in exchange rates for those currencies will give rise to exchange gains or losses, which results in direct foreign currency exposure for the unit. The functional currency concepts of translating a local (functional) currency into a company's reporting currency are relevant if the foreign currency exposure being hedged relates to any of the following:[5]

1. An unrecognized foreign-currency-denominated firm commitment.
2. A recognized foreign-currency-denominated asset or liability.
3. A foreign-currency-denominated forecasted transaction.
4. The forecasted functional-currency-equivalent cash flows associated with a recognized asset or liability.
5. A net investment in a foreign operation.

If the hedged item is denominated in a foreign currency, an entity may designate any of the following types of hedges of foreign currency exposure:

1. A fair value hedge of an unrecognized firm commitment or a recognized asset or liability (including an available-for-sale security).[5]
2. A cash flow hedge of any of the following:
   a. A forecasted transaction.
   b. An unrecognized firm commitment.
   c. The forecasted functional-currency-equivalent cash flows associated with a recognized asset or liability.
   d. A forecasted intra-entity transaction.
3. A hedge of a net investment in a foreign operation.

Accounting guidance that permits a recognized foreign-currency-denominated asset or liability to be the hedged item in a fair value or cash flow hedge of foreign currency exposure also pertains to a recognized foreign-currency-denominated receivable or payable that results from a hedged forecasted foreign-currency-denominated sale or purchase on credit. Specifically, an entity may choose to designate either of the following:[6]

1. A single cash flow hedge that encompasses the variability of functional currency cash flows attributable to foreign exchange risk related to the settlement of the foreign-currency-denominated receivable or payable resulting from a forecasted sale or purchase on credit.
2. Both of the following separate hedges:
   a. A cash flow hedge of the variability of functional currency cash flows attributable to foreign exchange risk related to a forecasted foreign-currency-denominated sale or purchase on credit.
   b. A foreign currency fair value hedge of the resulting recognized foreign-currency-denominated receivable or payable.

Assessing Hedge Effectiveness

In order for a company to qualify for the special accounting for hedges that defers the gain on the derivative instrument and the hedged item so that they are recorded on the financial statements in the same reporting period, the derivative used must be "highly effective" in offsetting changes in fair value or cash flows on the risk being hedged.[7] The difficulty for companies is that accounting standard setters do not define what is meant by highly effective. Fortunately, accounting practice has developed meaningful guidance to assist companies in qualifying for hedge accounting. High effectiveness testing compares the change in the fair value of the derivative instrument as scaled by the change in the fair value of the hedged item. Accounting guidance has accepted that if the change in the fair value of the derivative when compared to the change in the fair value of the hedged item results in a ratio of between 80% and 125% then the hedge is deemed highly effective at inception. This calculation would be computed at each company reporting date to ensure continued high effectiveness. The hedge effectiveness test always puts the change in the fair value of the derivative in the numerator and the change in fair value of the hedged item always in the denominator.

For example, assume we write a forward contract on inventory in order to protect the company from price increases (market risk) when we need to purchase the inventory. The value of the inventory is $100 at the time we write the forward contract. Assume the inventory spot price increases to $108 and the fair value change in the derivative is $10. Working the highly effective test, we get $10/$8 = 125%. Now, let's reverse the changes to the derivative and the hedged item inventory. The inventory increases by $10 and the fair value change in the derivative is $8. Now, the calculation is $8/$10 = 80%.

Accounting guidance requires that the hedging instrument must be highly effective both at the inception of the hedge and on an ongoing basis over the life of the hedge. It further requires that effectiveness tests be performed whenever financial statements or earnings are reported, at least every three months. In addition, accounting guidance requires that the hedge effectiveness assessments be done both prospectively (inception of the hedging arrangement) and retrospectively (look back over the life of the hedge in determining that the highly effective criteria is met).

Companies can select the methodology used to measure hedge effectiveness. The most common approach is to use the *dollar-offset* approach. This approach measures the change in fair value of the derivative instrument (fair value hedge) or changes in the present value of cash flows (cash flow hedge) against the change in the fair value of the hedged item (fair value hedge) or changes in the present value of cash flows of the hedged item (cash flow hedge).

The dollar-offset method can be used in performing the prospective and retrospective evaluation. The dollar-offset method is the only method that can be used in recognizing hedge ineffectiveness in the income statement. In addition to documenting the dollar-offset method as the measurement device that will be used to determine hedging effectiveness; companies must also choose whether effectiveness evaluation will be done for each reporting period (discrete) or over the life of the derivative instrument (cumulative).

The following example illustrates an application of the *dollar-offset analysis* for determining hedge effectives at inception and subsequent to inception. When reviewing the example, note the difference in qualifying for hedge accounting between documenting at inception the measure based on discrete or cumulative differences between the hedged item and the hedging instrument.[8]

Companies can also use regression analysis in assessing hedge effectiveness. Regression analysis is based on the mathematical equation $Y = a + b(x)$. In accounting for derivatives, the equation would translate to: Y being the independent variable (derivative instrument) and X being the dependent variable. We are trying to determine how much of the change in Y is explained by the change in X, with b being the notional. For example, let's assume that Y is a futures contract to purchase inventory. Assuming that b is equal to zero, and then X is the change in what it would cost the company to purchase inventory at the spot price on a reporting date. We would take the notional (bushels of wheat) and multiply that by the spot price on the reporting date. We would then compare that amount to the notional times the forward rate on the reporting date and determine if the change in Y (derivative instrument) is correlated closely to the change in spot rate within the 80% to 120% in determining effectiveness However, since companies must use dollar-offset analysis in making their accounting entries for their financial statements that is the methodology that is employed throughout this book. Companies that want to use regression analysis for hedge effectives testing are advised to purchase a detailed book on statistical analysis.

Table 2.2. *Assessing Hedge Effectiveness Table*

End of	Derivative*	Change	Hedged Item	Change	Discrete (%)	Cumulative (%)
Inception	0	0	0	0		
Quart. 1	50	50	(50)	(50)	100	100
Quart. 2	105	55	(107)	(57)	96	98
Quart. 3	129	24	(120)	(13)	185	108
Quart. 4	115	(14)	(116)	4	350	99

*Represents either the change in the fair value or the change in the present value of the expected future cash flows of the hedged item.

The Special Case of Interest Rate Swaps

Accounting guidance for interest rate swaps when determining effectiveness of the derivative instrument in offsetting fair value changes to the debt allows a company to assume perfect effectiveness provided:[9]

1. The notional amount of the swap matches the principal amount of the interest-bearing debt.
2. The fair value of the swap at inception is zero.
3. The formula for computing net settlements under the interest-rate swap is the same for each net settlement. This means that the fixed rate is the same throughout the term of the swap and debt and the variable rate is based on the same index (U.S. LIBOR) and includes the same constant adjustment or no adjustment.
4. The interest-bearing debt is not prepayable. (This is the requirement that is the most difficult to adhere to because holders of debt value the prepayment option depending on the movement of interest rates in capital markets.)
5. The expiration date of the swap matches the maturity date of the interest-bearing debt.
6. There is no floor or ceiling on the variable interest rate of the swap.
7. The interval between repricings of the variable interest rate in the swap is frequent enough to justify an assumption that the variable payment is at a market rate. This requirement in practice has generally come to mean 3 to 6 months.

This effectiveness test assessment for interest-rate swaps is termed the critical terms match. The use of this methodology for determining perfect effectiveness for the derivative instrument and the hedged item can be used for any hedging transaction at the inception of the hedge. In other words, when the critical terms match with the derivative instrument and the hedged item matches at inception of the hedge, the hedge would be deemed highly effective. For other than interest rate swaps, however, it still requires an effectiveness assessment over the life of the hedge.

The accounting rules for these initial and ongoing assessments are listed below for fair value and cash flow hedges.[10]

If a fair value hedge or a cash flow hedge initially qualifies for hedge accounting, the company would continue to assess whether the hedge meets the effectiveness test and also would measure any ineffectiveness during the hedge period. If the hedge fails the effectiveness test at any time (that is, if the entity does not expect the hedge to be highly effective at achieving offsetting changes in fair values or cash flows), the hedge ceases to qualify for hedge accounting. At least quarterly, the hedging entity shall determine whether the hedging relationship has been highly effective in having achieved offsetting changes in fair value or cash flows through the date of the periodic assessment. That assessment can be based on regression or other statistical analysis of past changes in fair values or cash flows as well as on other relevant information.

If an entity elects at the inception of a hedging relationship to use the same regression analysis approach for both prospective considerations and retrospective evaluations of assessing effectiveness, then during the term of that hedging relationship both the following conditions shall be met:

1. Those regression analysis calculations shall generally incorporate the same number of data points.
2. That entity must periodically update its regression analysis (or other statistical analysis).

Electing to use a regression or other statistical analysis approach instead of a dollar-offset approach to perform retrospective evaluations of assessing hedge effectiveness may affect the ability of an entity to apply hedge accounting for the current assessment period.

CHAPTER 3

Accounting for Fair Value Hedges

About This Chapter

Fair value hedges are used to hedge price risk on existing assets, liabilities, and firm commitments. Companies that use a fair value hedge want to manage the price risk of the change in fair value of the hedged item. Derivative instruments are useful in unlocking price risk due to the changing market conditions that will impact the value of the existing asset, liability, or firm commitment.

Accounting for fair value hedges results in recording in the financial statements the fair value of the derivative instrument for each reporting period and the changes in the fair value of the hedged item. These offsetting amounts, provided the hedge is highly effective, are recorded on the balance sheet with the offset amounts being recorded in the income statement.

Given the complexity of accounting for derivatives and to facilitate understanding of the economic impacts on the company's financial statement, this chapter will include three comprehensive examples of fair value hedges. These examples are designed to also illustrate the extensive documentation required for hedging activities as well as their impact on the financial statements.

Accounting Mechanics

Accounting guidance requires that companies recognize in the income statement for each reporting period (with the offset entry on the balance sheet) the changes in fair value of the derivative instrument as they occur for each reporting date (quarterly), as gains and losses from the derivative instrument that are used to hedge price risk. In addition, changes in the fair value of the existing asset, liability, or firm commitment are also recorded in the income statement as an adjustment to the carrying amount of the hedged item.

This adjustment of existing assets, liabilities, or a firm commitment that are designated as the hedged item is one of the more dramatic features of accounting for derivatives. Once a derivative is used to unlock the price risk for the hedged item in a fair value hedge, then accounting guidance for the hedged item is overridden and the changes in fair value are recorded in the balance sheet and in the income statement. For example, a Company wants to protect the carrying value of future purchases of inventory in order to protect itself from decreasing gross margins (sales minus cost of sales). The Company enters into a firm commitment to purchase inventory in three months and simultaneously purchases a forward contract to purchase inventory in three-months for the same notional amount as the firm commitment at the three month forward price. If the forward price rises above the amount of the forward contractual price, the derivative is in the money and recorded as an asset with the offset being a gain on hedging. For the firm commitment, since the fair value change would be to purchase the inventory at the new forward price, the company would record a loss on the firm commitment and record a liability.

These adjustments to the carrying value of the hedged item in a fair value hedge must be accounted for as any other adjustment of the carrying amount of an asset or liability. Using the aforementioned example, when the inventory is acquired by the company, the firm commitment (which could be an asset or a liability) would be included in the cost of the inventory and in the company's cost of sales computation similar to any other adjustment to the cost of the inventory.

The remainder of the chapter explores the economics, accounting, and documentation requirements for three common types of hedges. These hedges will involve: (a) an interest rate swap in which we are "protecting" the fair value of the existing debt, (b) using a futures contract to hedge the fair value of an existing asset inventory, and (c) hedging a firm commitment to purchase inventory by using forward contracts.

Because of the complexity of accounting for derivatives, the economic and accounting impacts on a company's financial statements are best understood by working systematically through comprehensive illustrations. For our purposes, I have chosen the most common derivative instruments (swaps, futures, and forward contracts) that are used to hedge an existing asset, liability, or firm commitment. All of the illustrations follow a format that allows for an examination for of each of the hedging transactions as a fully developed example that will serve as a standalone document, for that particular type of hedge. The format deployed for fair value hedges, cash flow hedges (Chapter 4), and foreign currency hedges (Chapter 5) is as follows:

1. *Description of the hedge transaction*, including the company's risk management strategy.
2. Narrative about the hedging transaction that includes all relevant requirements for companies in adhering to the accounting guidance rules for *hedge documentation*.
   a. Risk Management Strategy
   b. Hedging instrument
   c. Hedged item
   d. Assessing hedge effectiveness
3. Detailed *accounting treatment of the hedge* over the contractual term on the company's financial statements, including extensive explanations of the both the mathematics as well as accounting.
4. Detailed tables of the *financial statement impacts* of the hedges over the contractual term of the hedging arrangement.

Fair Value Hedge of Fixed-Rate Debt Using an Interest Rate Swap[1]

1. Description of the Hedge Transaction

On June 30, 20X1, a Manufacturing Company (Company) borrows $10,000,000 of three-year 7.5% fixed-rate debt. The debt is due at maturity and contains no prepayment option. Company, at the same time, enters into a three-year interest rate swap with a Finance Company to convert the debt's fixed rate to a variable (or floating) rate.

Under the terms of the swap, the Company receives interest at a fixed rate of 7.5% and agrees to pay interest at a variable rate equal to six-month U.S. London Interbank Offer Rate (LIBOR), based on the notional amount of $10,000,000. Both the debt and the swap require that payments be made or received on December 31 and June 30.

> *Note*: For illustrative purposes, we will only account for the two semiannual interest periods for this interest rate swap. For an interest rate swap in which the critical terms match, accounting guidance allows companies to treat the hedge as a perfect hedge. The entries then for the remaining life of the swap will perfectly offset in earnings.

The six-month U.S. LIBOR rate on each reset date determines the variable portion of the interest rate swap for the following six-month period. The Company designates the swap as a fair value hedge of the fixed rate debt, with changes in fair value that are due to changes in the benchmark rate which is U.S. LIBOR being the specific risk that is being hedged.

2. Hedge Documentation

a. *Risk Management Strategy*
   The objective of entering into the hedge is to protect the debt due to changes in fair value due to changes in the benchmark interest rate. Changes in the fair value of the swap are expected to be perfectly effective in offsetting changes in the fair value of the debt attributable to changes in the U.S. LIBOR swap rate, the designated benchmark interest rate.

b. *Hedging Instrument*
   $10,000,000 notional amount, receive fixed at 7.5% and pay variable at U.S. LIBOR, dated June 30, 20X1, with semi annual payments due on December 31 and June 30 ending on June 30, 20X4.

c. *Hedged Item*
   $10,000,000 three-year note payable on June 30, 20X4

d. *Assessing Hedge Effectiveness*

Because the critical terms of the hedging instrument and the hedged item match (i.e., principal and notional, reset dates and interest payment dates, and maturity of the note payable and of the swap), the hedge will be considered to be perfectly effective against changes in the fair value of the debt due to changes in the benchmark interest rate (U.S. LIBOR) over its term. The hedge is constructed as a perfect hedge, so there will be no need to assess the ineffectiveness over the term of the hedge. (Accounting guidance only allows no ongoing assessment of hedging effectiveness for interest rate swaps in which the critical terms match between the derivative instrument and the hedged item.)

Accounting guidance to qualify as a perfect hedge for an interest rate swap requires that companies perform the following steps.[1]

- Determine the difference between the fixed rate to be received on the swap and the fixed rate to be paid on the debt.
- Combine the difference with the variable rate to be paid on the swap.
- Compute and recognize interest expense using the combined-rate and fixed-rate debt's principal amount. For the interest-rate swap hedge above, the table would be as follows.

(*Note*: For illustration purposes, we will only use the December 30, 20X1 and the June 30, 20X2 interest payments.)

Table 3.1. Framework for Determining Interest Expense

Semiannual period ending	(a) Difference between fixed rates[1]	(b) Variable rate on the swap (%)	(c) Sum of (a) + (b) (%)	(d) Debt's principal amount ($)	(e) Semiannual interest expense (c) × (d)/2 ($)
12/30/X1	0.00%	6.00	6.00	10,000,000	300,000
06/30/X2	0.00%	7.00	7.00	10,000,000	350,000

[1]Note for (a) the computation is 7.5% on debt on notes payable and 7.50% on receive fixed from counterparty.

- Determine the fair value of the interest rate swap.

Table 3.2. Fair value of the Derivative Instrument

Date	Six-month U.S. LIBOR rate[1] (%)	Swap fair value asset (liability)[2] ($)	Debt fair value ($)
06/30X1	6.00	-0-[3]	(10,000,000)
12/31/x1	7.00	(323,000)	(9,677,000)
06/30/X2	5.5	55,000	(10,055,000)

[1]All rate changes take place on the date indicated.
[2]These fair values are assumed to be subsequent to the net swap settlements for the period, and were obtained by dealer quotes.
[3]Swap has zero value at inception because the underlying U.S. LIBOR has not changed. It is the change in the underlying that puts the swap in the money (asset) or out of the money (liability).

- Adjust the carrying amount of the swap to its fair value in the financial statements as well as the carrying amount of the note payable by an offsetting amount at each payment date and reporting date for the financial statements.

3. Accounting Treatment of the Hedging Instrument and the Hedged Item over the Contractual Term of the Hedge

The following financial statement analysis will illustrate all the accounting entries of the debt and the derivative instrument up to June 30, 20X2.

Table 2.3. Financial Statement Template

Assets =	Liabilities +	Stockholder's equity
		+ revenue (gain) − expense (loss)

June 30, 20X1
To record the issuance of debt

Assets =	Liabilities +	Stockholder's equity
+ Cash + 10,000,000	+ Debt + 10,000,000	

December 31, 20X1

To record the semiannual interest expense on the principal at the fixed rate of 7.5%

Assets =	Liabilities +	Stockholder's equity
– Cash – 375,000		– Interest expense – 375,000

Note: Companies that are doing an interest rate swaps, will, of course, still make interest payments to their debt holders. The derivative instrument is designed to mitigate the impact of interest rate risk on the fair value of the debt. The contractual relationship between the company (receive fixed—pay variable) and the counterparty (receive variable—pay fixed) will determine the amount to be net settled and will therefore determine the net interest expense to be recorded by the company.

To record the change in the fair value of the derivative instrument at the end of 1st reporting period.

Assets =	Liabilities +	Stockholder's equity
	+ Swap contract + 323,000	– Loss on hedge – 323,000

Note that U.S. LIBOR resets to 7%, which causes the derivative to go out of the money and will be recorded as a liability with the offset entry a loss on hedge account income statement.

To record change in the debt's fair value that is attributable to changes in interest rates at the end of 1st reporting period for changes in U.S. LIBOR from 6 to 7%.

Assets =	Liabilities +	Stockholder's equity
	– Debt – 323,000	+ Gain on hedge + 323,000

Note: Since the critical terms of the debt and the derivative instrument as regards notional of the derivative and principal of the debt and maturity date and settlement date of the derivative match the interest-rate swap is considered in accounting guidance to be a perfect hedge. The decrease in the debt account is offset by a gain on hedge which will offset the loss on the hedge recorded for the swap. The financial statement effects will net out to zero. The income statement records the loss on hedge and the gain on hedge in the same account and the swap contract liability is offset by the decrease in the debt by the same amount. There is no net change in the income statement or on the liability section of the balance sheet. This is because the swap contract liability amount that will increase current liabilities is offset by decrease in the debt account by the same amount.

To record the settlement of the semiannual swap amount receivable at 7.5%, minus the amount payable at U.S. LIBOR at 6%.

Assets =	Liabilities +	Stockholder's equity
+ Cash + 75,000		+ Interest expense + 75,000

Note: Company pays variable at 6% resulting in net interest expense of $75,000 ($375,000 − $300,000) and is entitled to receive fixed interest payments of $375,000. Since all interest rate swap payments are net settled, the company records the $75,000 and reduces the interest expense account on the income statement.

When working through the mathematics of the impact on the financial statements of the hedge transaction, remember that we compute the fair value of the debt and the derivative instrument based on the reset amounts on the reset date (7% on December 31, 20X1). The amount of net interest expense recorded by the company is computed using the interest rate at the beginning of the reporting period (6% U.S. LIBOR on June 30, 20X1, compared to receive fixed at 7.5%).

June 30, 20X2
To record interest expense at the semiannual interest expense on the debt principal at 7.5%.

Assets =	Liabilities +	Stockholder's equity
− Cash − 375,000		− Interest expense − 375,000

To record the change in the debt's fair value that is attributable to changes in interest rates at the end of the 2nd reporting period incorporating the change in U.S. LIBOR from 7 to 5.5%.

Assets =	Liabilities +	Stockholder's equity
	+ Debt + 378,000	− Loss on hedge − 378,000

Note: The debt will have a balance of $1,055,000 on the balance sheet.

To record the change in fair value of the swap contract at the end of the company's 2nd reporting period resulting in changes in U.S. LIBOR.

Assets =	Liabilities +	Stockholder's equity
+ Swap contract + 378,000		+ Gain on hedge + 378,000

Note: The swap contract at the end of reporting period 1 was a liability. However, the movement of interest rates below the original U.S. LIBOR of 6% puts the derivative in the money. Also, the swap contract has moved from a liability balance to an asset balance of $55,000 on the balance sheet (−$323,000 − $378,000).

To record the net settled payment at 7.5% less U.S. LIBOR at 7%.

Assets =	Liabilities +	Stockholder's equity
+ Cash + 25,000		+ Interest expense + 25,000

Assets =	Liabilities +	Stockholder's equity
		+ Interest expense + 25,000

Note: Derivative instrument is net settled resulting in net interest expense being $350,000 ($375,000 − $25,000)

4. Financial Statement Impacts over the Contractual Term

Note: The following table summarizes the financial statement impacts of accounting for the interest rate swap. The format of the analysis follows the illustration of accounting entries that impact the financial statements that we have used earlier. Balance sheet values represent cumulative amounts.

Financial Statement Effects

Date/Accounts balance sheet	+ Asset =	Liabilities +	Shareholder's equity
June 30, 20X1			
Cash	+ 10,000,000		
Debt		+ 10,000,000	
December 31, 20X1			
Cash	+ 9,700,000		
Swap contract		+ 323,000	
Debt		+ 9,677,000	
Retained earnings (Interest expense)			– 300,000
June 30, 20X2			
Cash	+ 9,350,000		
Swap contract	+ 55,000		
Debt		+ 10,055,000	
Retained earnings (Interest expense)			– 650,000
Dates/Accounts income statement			
December 31, 20X1			
Interest expense			– 300,000
June 30, 20X1			
Interest expense			– 350,000
Total impact on the income statement			– 650,000

The interest rate swap example illustrates the use of a derivative instrument that "attaches" itself to an existing liability. The next illustration will use an existing asset and deploy the use of a futures contract to hedge the fair value of inventory. Normally, for hedges of existing assets using futures contracts, there would normally be some ineffectiveness between the derivative instrument and the hedged item. This occurs because the forward (futures) price is determined by the spot price (price at which you could purchase the commodity and take possession), which tends to change daily. On futures markets there is a mathematical equivalence between the spot rate and the futures rate. The spot rate, for any particular trading day, times 1 + r^t = future price. The formula is: the spot rate is multiplied by 1 × the risk-free rate, with ^{t} representing the time to expiration of the futures contract. Therefore, after inception the spot rate can move with will change the futures rate over the life of the contractual arrangement.

In addition, futures contracts for commodities may contain basis adjustments for location, transportation, and storage costs.

The following example is designed to illustrate the documentation and the financial statement impacts of a *fair value hedge of commodity inventory using futures contracts.*

On October 1, X1, Montana Mining Company has 10,000,000 pounds of copper inventory on hand at an average cost of $0.65 per pound. To protect the inventory from a decline in copper prices, the company hedges its position by selling 400 copper contracts on the Chicago futures exchange for commodities. The exchange requires that each copper contract be for 25,000 pounds so the company sells 400 contracts at the futures price of $0.93 per pound for delivery in February 20, X2. This delivery date coincides with the company's expected physical sale of the copper.

The company is hedging changes in the fair value of its copper inventory order to protect its gross margins (sales minus its inventory cost when sold). The margin deposit (explained as follows) for each copper contract is $700. The spot price of copper on October 1, X1, is $0.91. The spot price on December 31, 20X1, is $0.89 and the futures price on that date is $0.91.

On February 20, X2, the Company closes out its futures contract by entering into an offsetting contract in which it agrees to buy 400 February copper contracts at $0.92 per pound. (On settlement date, the spot and futures will converge to the same $0.92 per pound.)

The Company sells the copper in the open market on February 20, X2, at $0.92 per pound.

Note: Margin deposits for futures contracts are necessary as the exchange guarantees that both sides will deliver under the contractual arrangement. In addition, futures contracts generally require cash payments from the party out of the money to the party who is in the money for all trading days. The amount is kept in the margin account of the company during the life of the hedge to insure sufficient cash is available should the derivative instrument go out of the money which would require a cash transfer of cash to a counterparty. Payments to the futures exchange for margin accounts when executing a derivative contract creates an asset for the company, normally called futures contracts. All subsequent changes in the derivative instrument (futures contract) are entered into the futures contract account. On the settlement date of the derivative instrument, the futures account will be paid in cash by the exchange when there is an asset balance or be paid in cash to the exchange when there is a liability balance.

The following table summarizes the spot and futures price for the reporting and settlement dates of the derivative instrument and the hedged item.

Chicago Exchange Copper Prices

Date	Spot	Futures
October 1, X1	$0.91	$0.93
December 31, X1	$0.89	$0.91
February 20, X2	$0.92	$0.92

Risk Management Strategy

In order to protect the fair value of the inventory from price declines on the sale of the copper the company enters into a futures contract on the Chicago exchange by selling 400 copper contracts at $0.93 for delivery on February 20, X2, to match the expected sale of the copper. The company is hedging its commodity price exposure for the entire hedged asset (copper inventory), which also reflects the locational, transportation, and storage cost differences between Montana and Chicago (basis adjustments to the spot and futures price of copper on the different exchanges). Since, the Company is hedging the risk of changes in the existing asset inventory the company is using a fair value hedge. The Company expects that locational, transportation, and storage differences will represent some ineffectiveness in the hedge that will be recognized currently in earnings. The Company, however, expects the correlation between Montana spot and futures prices on copper and the spot and futures prices in Chicago to be highly effective in offsetting changes in fair value of the copper inventory located in Montana. Past historical evidence between the copper inventories, spot and futures prices in Montana have shown a high correlation with the spot and futures prices in Chicago over similar historical periods.

Hedging Instrument

Company sells 400 copper contracts, 25,000 pounds per contract, on the Chicago exchange, on October 1, X1, at $.93 per pound, for delivery on February 20, X2, which will be the same date the Company at the physical sale of the copper.

Hedged Item

Copper inventory, 10,000,000 pounds purchased at an average cost of $.65.

Assessing Hedge Effectiveness

The Company has historical data of the high correlation between the Montana market for copper and the Chicago market for copper. The company expects that the correlation will continue over the life of the hedge. The changes in fair value of futures contracts related to changes in the spot price of copper inventory on the Chicago exchange are expected to be highly effective in offsetting future changes in the fair value of copper inventory located in Montana.

The company will use changes in the fair value of the copper inventory attributable to changes in the spot price on the Chicago exchange. The company has determined that the hedging relationship will be highly effective at inception and over the life of the hedge at offsetting changes in fair value of the copper inventory attributable to the changes in the sport price of copper. The company documents the following hedge-effectiveness analysis.

Determining hedge effectiveness

Date	Chicago exchange copper (gain) loss	Inventory (gain) loss	Effectiveness ratio for the period
12/31/X1	$(200,000)[1]	$220,000[2]	0.91
2/20/X2	300,000[3]	(310,000)[3]	0.91

[1] 10,000,000 ($.89 − $.91)

[2] Company estimates the change of the fair value of inventory in Montana by starting with the Chicago exchange price change and adjusting for transportation and storage costs.

[3] 10,000,000 ($.92 − $.89)

Note: The analysis here indicates the effectiveness ratio is in an acceptable range of 80–120% of the derivative instrument's change in fair value when compared to the existing asset's (copper inventory) fair value, and therefore qualifies for under accounting standards for special hedge accounting treatment (200,000 / 220,000 = 91%). In addition, the ongoing hedge effectiveness analysis will use the change in the spot rate over the term of hedge in determining hedge effectiveness.

Note: the hedged item (inventory) fair value changes that will be recorded in the financial statements will be based on changes in the spot rate. The derivative instrument (futures contract) fair value changes that will be recorded in the financial statements will be based on changes in the futures rate.

The hedge effectiveness assessment is done on a spot-to-spot basis because the Company is hedging the fair value risk and an inventory price decrease. However, accounting guidance would require that the derivative instrument's fair value be based on changes in the futures price. This is because the fair value of the derivative instrument (futures contract) is determined by changes in the future rates of copper inventory.

Accounting for the Fair Value Hedge of Inventory

Financial Statement Template

Assets =	Liabilities +	Stockholder's equity
		+ Revenue (gain) − Expense (loss)

October 1, X1[1]

To record the margin deposit on 400 copper contracts

Assets =	Liabilities +	Stockholder's equity
+ Future contracts + 280000 − Cash − 280000		

At the inception of the hedging contract neither the derivative instrument nor the copper inventory has moved in or out of the money, because the underlying spot or futures rates have not moved.

Note: the futures contract account is an asset at inception that will be increased (asset) or decreased (decrease asset or the account becomes a liability) depending on whether the derivative instrument goes in the money (increase), which will be a payment to the company or out of the money (decrease). At the end of the arrangement, we will write off the futures contract account and collect or pay cash.

December 31, X1

To record gain on the derivative instrument with the offset entry to the futures contract account:

Assets =	Liabilities +	Stockholder's equity
+ Future contract + 200,000		+ Gain on hedge + 200,000

Assets =	Liabilities +	Stockholder's equity
		+ Gain on hedge + 200,000

Note: The mathematics of the gain on futures contract is computed using the February futures price and is illustrated in the following table.

February copper futures price on October 1, X1	$0.93
February copper futures price on December 31, X1	0.91
Gain per pound	0.02
Notional amount in pounds	10,000,000
Gain on futures contracts on December 31, X2	$200,000

To record the loss on hedge activity for the existing asset (inventory):

Assets =	Liabilities +	Stockholder's equity
– Copper inventory – 220,000		– Loss on hedge – 220,000

Note: The loss of hedge includes the $200,000 computed as 10,000,000 ($.91 − $.89) = $200,000. In addition, the $20,000 represents locational and transportation costs. The ineffectiveness portion of the hedge ($20,000) would go directly to the income statement.

February 20, X2

To record the loss on hedge activity of the derivative instrument:

Assets =	Liabilities +	Stockholders Equity
– Future contract – 100,000		– Loss on hedge – 100,000

Note: The mathematics of the gain on futures contract is computed using the February futures price and is illustrated in the following table. February 20, X2 is the settlement date.

Calculating Gain on the Futures Contract

February copper futures price on December 31, X1	$0.91
February copper futures price on February 20, X2	$0.92
Gain per pound	$0.01
Notional amount in pounds	10,000,000
Gain on futures contracts on February 20, X2	$100,000

To record the gain on hedge for the existing asset (inventory):

Assets =	Liabilities +	Stockholder's equity
+ Copper inventory + 310,000		+ Gain on hedge + 310,000

Note: The gain is the computation of 10,000,000 ($0.92 – $0.89) = $300,000 plus an additional gain of $10,000 due to locational and transportation adjustments.

To record the settlement of the futures contract and record the receipt of cash:

Assets =	Liabilities +	Stockholder's equity
+ Cash + 380,000 – Futures contract – 380,000		

Note: The futures contact computation is ($280,000 + $200,000) – $100,000 = $380,000

To record the sale of the 400 copper inventory:

Assets =	Liabilities +	Stockholder's equity
+ Cash + 9,200,000 – Copper inventory – 6,590,000		+ Revenue from sales + 9,200,000 – Expense from cost of sales – 6,590,000

Note: The cash amount above is based on 10,000,000 pounds ($0.92 spot rate on February 20, X2). The copper inventory amount is the agreement to purchase 400 February contracts at the spot price of $0.92 per pound.

The cost of sales and the copper inventory accounts result from:

Original cost of copper	$6,500,000
Adjustment at December 31, X1	– 220,000
Adjustment at February 20, X2	+ 100,000
Ending value	$6,590,000

Financial Statement Impact: Balance Sheet

Date/Accounts	Assets =	Liabilities +	Shareholder's equity
October 1, X1			
Cash	– 280,000		
Inventory	6,500,000		
Futures contract	+ 280,000		
Retained earnings			– 6,500,000
December 31, X1			
Cash	– 280,000		
Inventory	+ 6,280,000		
Futures contract	+ 480,000		
Retained earnings			– 6,480,000
February 20, X2			
Cash	+ 9,300,000		
Retained earnings			– 9,300,000

Note: The inventory balance on December 31, X1, is the result of the change in fair value of the hedged item from October 1, X1 ($220,000). The cash balance of $9,300,000 is the result of selling the copper inventory contracts at the spot price of $0.92 and receiving cash from the settlement of the futures contracts. The futures contracts, original cost was $280,000 and they were sold for $380,000 resulting in a cash of $100,000.

Financial Statement Impact: Income Statement

Dates/Accounts	Assets =	Liabilities +	Shareholder's equity + Gain – Loss
December 31, X1			
Loss on hedge			$–200,000
Gain on hedge			+ 220,000
Total			+ 20,000
February 20, X2			
Loss on hedge			– 100,000
Gain on hedge			+ 310,000
Gross margin on Sale of inventory			+ 2,610,000[1]
Total			+ 2,820,000
Cumulative income statement impact			$+2,800,000

Note: 1The gross margin is calculated as $9,200,000 sale price at February 20, X2, minus $6,590,000, which is the net carrying value of inventory on the same date.

Note: by entering into the futures contract the Company locked in a gross profit of $2,800,000, which represents the $0.93 less the $0.65 cost of the inventory on the 10,000,000 pounds of copper. Mission accomplished.

For our final comprehensive illustration in this chapter, we will demonstrate a *fair value hedge of a firm commitment using a forward contract.*

Silver Company (Company) is a manufacturer of silver jewelry. On July 1, X1, the Company enters into a firm commitment to purchase 1,000 troy ounces of silver on December 31, X1, at the current forward rate of $310 per troy ounce. The company enters into the firm commitment because its supplier requires a fixed price contract. However, the company would prefer to pay the market price at the time of delivery and record the silver inventory at whatever the market price will be on December 31, X1.

In order to accomplish their objective, the company enters into a six-month forward contract to sell 1,000 troy ounces of silver at the current forward rate of $310 per troy ounce. By entering into the forward contract, the company unlocks the firm commitment. The forward contract requires net cash settlement of December 31, X1, and has a fair value of zero at inception because the underlying forward rates and the firm commitment prices are equal at the inception of the forward contract.

Risk Management Strategy

The objective of the hedge is to protect the fair value of the firm commitment from changes in the market value of silver. The forward contract to sell 1,000 troy ounces of silver at the forward price of $310 per troy ounce on December 31, X1 is expected to be highly effective in offsetting changes in the fair value of the firm-hedged item. The firm commitment requires the company to purchase 1,000 troy ounces of silver at the forward price of $310 per troy ounce on December 31, X1. The company expects the forward price of silver over the life of the forward to decline and wants to purchase silver ounces at the market price on December 31, X1. (In this illustration, the firm commitment is not the derivative, but is instead the hedged item.)

Hedging Instrument

Six-month forward contract to sell 1,000 troy ounces of silver at $310 per troy ounce entered into on July 1, X1, with a settlement date of December 31, X1.

Hedged Item

Firm commitment to purchase 1,000 troy ounces of silver at the current forward rate of $310 per troy ounce on December 31, X1. The firm commitment does not qualify as a derivative in this arrangement.

Assessing Hedge Effectiveness

Hedge effectiveness both, at inception and over the life of the hedge, will be assessed based on the overall changes in the fair value of the contract, based on changes in the December 31, X1, forward price and changes in the fair value of the firm commitment, which is also based on changes in the forward price. The company will use the cumulative dollar-offset method to hedge effectiveness of the derivative instrument (forward contract to sell) and the firm commitment to buy 1,000 troy ounces of silver. At inception and over the life of the hedge since the critical terms of the firm commitment and the forward contract match such as dates, quantities, and the underlying commodity, the company expects the forward contract to be highly effective in offsetting changes in the overall fair value of the firm commitment. Any ineffectiveness from changes in the spot price for the required reporting periods and the December 31, X1, forward price will be reflected in the net income. The company prepares the following hedge effectiveness table in order to illustrate hedge effectiveness.

Note: The effectiveness documentation at the inception of the hedge and its ongoing effectiveness, in order to qualify for hedge accounting, would normally be done by using historical information about the offsetting changes in fair value between the derivative instrument and the hedged item. For our purposes, we are using a hypothetical example that mirrors the accounting for the hedging arrangement.

In practice, a company would gather evidence of the historical movement of prices of the derivative instrument based on changes in the underlying and changes in the fair value of the hedged item for a fair value hedge over an equivalent term of the hedge. The company would then create a "hypothetical" derivative that would mirror previous fair value changes in the derivative instruction and determine the degree of correlation in the changes to the fair value of the existing asset, liability, or firm commitment.

Hedge effectiveness documentation is performed to determine at inception if the derivative instrument and the hedged item's fair value changes are effective in offsetting fair value changes at the 80 to 125% level in order to make a determination as to whether or not the company qualifies for hedge accounting. The examples here treat the forecasted movement of the underlying, interest rates, futures prices, and forward prices, currency prices in order to demonstrate both the effectiveness of the hedge as well as the accounting and the impact on a company's financial statements.

Hedge Effectiveness Computations

Date	Spot price	Forward price for settlement on December 31, X1	Fair value of forward contract— asset	Fair value of firm commitment— liability	Effectiveness ratio
July 1, X1	$300	$310	–	–	–
September 30, X1	292	297	12,808[1]	12,808	100%
December 31, X1	285	285	25,000[2]	25,000	100%

[1]The fair value of the forward contract on September 30 is ($310 – 297) × 1000 ounces = $13,000. Since forward contracts are not exchange traded, accounting guidance would require the use of a discount rate from inception to the reporting period. Assuming a 6% discount, then $13,000/ (1+.015) =$12,808. (The 6% discount would be divided by 4 to determine the 1.5%.)
[2]The fair value of the forward contract for December 31 is ($310 – 285) × 1000 ounces = $25,000. Since this is the settlement date there would be no discount applied to the amount.

Note: The forward contract and the firm commitment are both valued using the forward rate and since the critical terms match there is no ineffectiveness in the hedge. In practice, similar to the copper inventory hedge there may be locational, transportation, or storage costs of a commodity that would result in some ineffectiveness between the hedged item and the derivative instrument when using a forward contract (this would be the case for a commodity that required physical delivery). However, in this hedge since we are hedging a firm commitment there are none of those costs. We will merely swap out the contracts on settlement date and buy the commodity at the spot price on the settlement date of delivery.

This illustration is principally designed to demonstrate the financial statement effects of hedging a firm commitment.

Accounting for the Fair Value Hedge of a Firm Commitment

Assets =	Liabilities +	Stockholder's equity
		+ Gain on hedge – Loss on hedge

July 1, X1

No financial statement effect on July 1, X1, because neither the firm commitment nor the forward contract has moved in or out of the money based on changes in the forward rates.

Note: Forward contracts generally do not require any upfront payments similar to what was illustrated in the previous example for futures contracts, which are exchange driver transactions. A forward contract is generally between a party and a counterparty and does not require the payment/ receipt of cash in a margin account.

Forward contracts, however, in the contractual terms between the parties in the transaction must include terms and conditions of the transaction that provide each party with a high level of reasonable assurance that each party will perform the contractual specifications. This is normally done by inserting penalty clauses for each party to the contract that are significant enough to assure each party performs under the contract.

The exception of not recording the financial statement impacts at inception of the contract occurs when the party and counterparty employ a 3rd party intermediary who arranges the forward contract for a fee. When that occurs, normally one party would pay the intermediary and record an asset for the payment made to the intermediary.

September 30, X1

To record the changes in fair value of the forward contract (derivative instrument) and the firm commitment (hedged item):

Assets =	Liabilities +	Stockholder's equity
+ Forward contract + 12,808		+ Gain on hedge + 12,808

Note: Forward contract is in the money because the forward price for December 31, X1, has decreased from $310 in July 1, X1, to $297 in September 30, X1. Since the contract "could" be net settled for $310 per ounce, we record a gain on hedge for the derivative instrument. The gain is discounted at 6% annual percentage rate (APR) for the 3 months.

To record changes in fair value of the firm commitment:

Assets =	Liabilities +	Stockholder's equity
	+ Firm commitment + 12,808	– Loss on Hedge – 12,808

Note: The fair value change in the firm commitment is a liability because the accounting guidance for the fair value hedge mandates a loss on the existing asset when there is a gain on the derivative instrument (forward contract). In addition, the company is required to have a fixed price purchase of silver at the forward July 1, X1 price for December 31, X1. The hedge accounting is matching the two parallel forward prices on the firm commitment and the forward contract in order to enable the company to purchase the silver inventory at the spot price on December 31, X1.

December 31, X1

To record the change in fair value of the forward contract:

Assets =	Liabilities +	Stockholder's equity
+ Forward contract + 12,192		+ Gain on hedge + 12,192

Note: The forward contract adds $12,192 in order to arrive at a balance sheet amount of $25,000 for the forward contract account. The $25,000 is arrived at by comparing the December 31, X1 forward value of $310 for the July 1, X1 forward December 31, X1 value and comparing it to the forward (and spot price) value on December 31, X1 of $285.

To record change in fair value for the firm commitment:

Assets =	Liabilities +	Stockholder's equity
	+ Firm commitment + 12,192	– Loss on hedge – 12,192

Note: The firm commitment computation of loss of hedge is the same as the computation for the derivative instrument (forward contract).

To record settlement of the forward contract:

Assets =	Liabilities +	Stockholder's equity
+ Cash + 25,000 – Forward contract – 25,000		

Note: Company cash settles the forward contract and removes the contract asset from its books. The $25,000 in cash results from the movement of the forward price from $310 – $285) × 1,000 ounces. The company now has $25,000 in cash from the movement of the forward prices to offset its cash purchase of the silver inventory for the firm commitment of $310 X 1,000 ounces = $310,000. This hedge places the company's cash flow for the hedge at $310,000 – $25,000 = $285,000. The company has therefore been able to purchase silver inventory at the market price, which was the risk management strategy they were pursuing.

To record the purchase of 1,000 ounces of silver at the contractual price for the firm commitment:

Assets =	Liabilities +	Stockholder's equity
+ Silver inventory + 310,000 – Cash – 310,000		

Note: For the firm commitment, company settles the contract by purchasing its silver inventory at the contract rate of $310.

To remove the firm commitment from the balance sheet and reduce the silver inventory account:

Assets =	Liabilities +	Stockholder's equity
– Silver inventory – 25,000	– Firm commitment – 25,000	

Note: The Company's firm commitment account mirrors the changes to the forward contract. The logic of the accounting for a firm commitment (or existing asset or liability) in a fair value hedge should now be clarified. The firm commitment liability is written off against the inventory account reducing its balance to $285,000. The company's risk management strategy of protecting itself from paying the forward price on July 1, X1, for December forward rates has been accomplished.

CHAPTER 4

Cash Flow Hedges

About This Chapter

Cash flow hedges are designed to lock in variable (floating) future expected cash flows of an anticipated or forecasted transaction. To review, fair value hedges convert fixed cash flows on an existing asset, liability, or firm commitment to variable cash flows and protect the hedged item's fair value. For cash flow hedges the opposite is true; the company takes inherently variable forecasted cash flows and converts them to fixed cash flows. Cash flow hedges are designed as a hedge of the variable cash flows from a forecasted transaction that is expected to occur in the future.

This chapter will discuss the use of cash flow hedges that companies can use to manage their risk exposure given the relative uncertainty of forecasting operating and financial transactions that will change future cash flows for the company. Derivative instruments used in cash flow hedges can reduce the uncertainty, for companies, of the amount of cash to be received or paid for operating and financial transactions.

The chapter will conclude with three comprehensive examples that will illustrate the economics and financial statement impacts of cash flow hedges.

Forecasted (Anticipated) Transactions

Forecasted transactions are eligible for cash flow hedge accounting, while firm commitments are only eligible for fair value hedge accounting. Accounting guidance defines forecasted transactions as *probable* future transactions that do not meet the definition of a firm commitment (which are only permissible for fair value hedges). Forecasted transactions can be contractually established or merely probable because of a company's past or expected business practices. As discussed previously, for a contract to meet the definition of a firm commitment, all of its relevant terms must be contractually fixed (e.g., price, quantity, timing, interest, or exchange rate) and the performance must be contractually required. On the other hand, in a forecasted transaction, either some term of the transaction is variable or the transaction is not contractually certain. Therefore, the distinguishing characteristic between a forecasted transaction and a firm commitment is the certainty and enforceability of the terms of the transaction.[1]

Because hedging a firm commitment and hedging a forecasted transaction give rise to different risk exposures, companies will need to deploy different risk management derivative instruments to accomplish their risk management strategies for the forecasted cash flows. For example, when hedging a firm commitment the company's goal is to unlock the fixed price position and pay the variable (market) price. For the hedge of a forecasted transaction the company would use derivative instruments to "fix" the amount of cash flows paid or received.

As discussed in Chapter 2, hedge documentation is vital in qualifying for hedge accounting. This documentation can be particularly perplexing for forecasted transactions. The difficulty is in meeting the standard setter's guidance that the transaction is probable of occurring. Accounting guidance for derivatives would indicate that the standard setters interpret probable at a high level, normally greater than or equal to a 75% probability of occurring. Useful guidelines when documenting the hedge include:

- Be very specific as to the date, or the period within which, the forecasted transaction will occur
- Try to be as specific as possible concerning the nature of the asset or liability from which the future cash flows will be derived
- Nail down the expected currency or the physical quantity to be delivered or purchased from the forecasted transaction

Accounting for Cash Flow Hedges

The effective portion of the gain or loss on a derivative instrument designated as a cash flow hedge is reported in other comprehensive income, and the ineffective portion is reported in earnings. The derivative instrument is carried at fair value of the balance sheet. However, unlike fair value hedges, since the hedged item is a forecasted transaction there is no existing asset, liability, or firm on which to "wash" out the transaction from the income statement. Cash flow hedge accounting will record the offset fair value change in the derivative instrument in a shareholder's equity account called Other Comprehensive Income (OCI). It is this arbitrary accounting that makes cash flow hedge accounting difficult to understand. Until the hedge is settled it is difficult for the company to determine the hedge effectiveness as shown of the financial statements over the contractual term of the hedge.

Amounts in other comprehensive income (OCI) shall be reclassified into earnings in the same period or periods during which the hedged forecasted transaction affects earnings (e.g., when a forecasted sale actually occurs). If the hedged transaction results in the acquisition of an asset or the incurrence of a liability, the gains and losses in accumulated other comprehensive income shall be reclassified into earnings in the same period or periods during which the asset acquired or liability incurred affects earnings (such as in the periods that depreciation expense, interest expense, or cost of sales is recognized).

This requirement, for recording interest expense over the term of the debt or recording depreciation expense over the useful life of the equipment purchases mandates that companies carefully track the hedge transaction over its entire contractual life, including the life of the "hedged item". For example, if your cash flow hedge results in a purchase of machinery with a 10-year life the related OCI account in shareholder equity will be released to earnings over a 10-year period of time. This requirement substantially increases the documentation for companies using cash flow hedge derivatives.

Assessing Hedge Effectiveness

In order to qualify for hedge accounting, the hedge relationship must be expected to be highly effective at inception and on an ongoing basis throughout the term of the hedging relationship. However, determining the extent to which a cash flow hedge is ineffective is more complicated than in a fair value hedge where both the derivative and the hedged item are adjusted for changes in fair value (with respect to the hedged risk) through earnings. This complication develops because the "hedged item" is anticipated or forecast cash flows which may diverge from the changes in the fair value of the derivative instrument because of changing economic conditions of the forecasted transaction.

Cash flow hedges use the same effectiveness methodologies as used by fair value hedges. Most common is the dollar-offset approach whereby the change in the derivative instrument is compared to the change in the hedged item. Hedged transactions will qualify for the special hedge accounting when the changes between the two values are in the 80% to 125% effectiveness range. The major difference in determining hedge effectiveness is the calculation of the fair value change in the forecasted expected future cash flows. The preferred measurement methodology in determining the "hedged item" side of the formula in performing effectiveness tests is to determine the expected present value of future cash flows for the hedged transaction.

Hedges of cash flow exposures often involve a component of the total cash flow that is the source of its variability. Considering the source of variability in a hedged cash flow is one of the first steps in assessing ineffectiveness of a cash flow hedge. For example, if the hedged forecasted transaction is the variable interest payment on a debt obligation whose contractual terms provide for the payment of interest at the prime interest rate plus a fixed spread, changes in the prime interest rate are the only source of variability of the forecasted cash flow.

In situations where the variability of the hedged cash flow is solely attributable to changes in an interest rate index, ineffectiveness may be assessed solely by considering the effectiveness of the derivative in offsetting changes resulting from changes in the index. As a result, when the designated derivative is based on the same interest rate index as the cause of the variability of the hedged cash flow, and the other terms of the exposure and the derivative match, then we have a "perfect hedge. However, unlike the exception in the fair value hedge that ongoing effectiveness need not be assessed, for cash flow hedges ineffectiveness after hedge inception must always be assessed to determine any ineffectiveness. This assessment is done because any ineffectiveness goes directly to earnings while the highly effective portion of the hedge goes to an OCI account in the shareholder's equity.

Similar to a fair value hedge when the critical terms match for the derivative instrument and the "hedged item" (forecasted cash flows) then at inception the company can assume that the hedge will be highly effective (changes in the derivative fair value will offset changes in fair value of the forecasted transaction). Critical terms would consist of the timing of the transaction, quantities of a commodity, and delivery dates. However, since the critical terms of the forecasted transaction can change as to timing and amounts, companies need to carefully monitor the critical terms match on an ongoing basis in determining any ineffectiveness which would be charged to earnings in the period under measurement which for derivative instruments is every three months.

Forecasted transactions may be based on the company's historical experience, say of revenue projections for a particular region. At inception, the company could design a derivative instrument that matched their revenue expectations. However, generally as the settlement date gets closer the estimates of revenue are likely to change causing ineffectiveness in the hedging relationship.

Because the hedged item is forecasted cash flows, accounting guidance limits the amount that is recorded in OCI. The cash flow hedging model requires that companies determine if the change in fair value of the derivative instrument as compared to the change in fair value of the forecasted future cash flows represents an "underhedge" or an "overhedge". An "underhedge" occurs when the cumulative change in the fair value of the derivative instrument is equal to or less than necessary to offset the cumulative change in expected future cash flows of the hedged item. When this is the case the entire change in the fair value of the derivative is recorded in OCI, and there is no ineffectiveness in earnings. However, if the cumulative change in the fair value of the derivative instrument is greater than the cumulative change in the fair value of expected future cash flows, then the amount in excess is changed to earnings with the remainder going to OCI in shareholder's equity.

The following example on Measuring Hedge Effectiveness[1] will be used to illustrate how to apply the accounting guidance for effectiveness measures for cash flow hedges. Company has designated the overall change in cash flows related to the forecasted transaction as the hedged risk. However, because of differences between the derivative instrument and the hedged item, some ineffectiveness is expected to occur. The example will first construct a table demonstrating the hedge effectiveness assessment, then provides the accounting impact on the financial statements, and finally provide a detailed examination of the OCI account on the balance sheet.

Measuring Hedge Effectiveness

Reading the Table

A—Fair value change in the derivative during the period with decreases in fair value shown by using (parentheses)

B—Cumulative change in the fair value of the derivative

C—Present value of expected future cash flows from the hedged transaction for the period with decreases shown by (parentheses)

D—Cumulative change in the present value of the expected future cash flows

E—Lesser of the two cumulative changes

F—Adjustment made to OCI

Computations represented by the table:

1. Determine the change in the fair value of the derivative and the change in the present values of the hedged transaction. (columns A & C)
2. Determine the cumulative changes in the fair value of the derivative and the cumulative changes in the present values of the cash flows of the hedged transaction. (columns B&B)
3. Determine the lesser of the absolute values of the two accounts in #2 above. (column E)

Measuring Hedge Effectiveness

Period	A	B	C	D	E	F
1	$100	$100	$(96)	$(96)	$96	$96
2	94	194	(101)	(197)	194	98
3	(162)	32	160	(37)	32	(162)
4	(101)	(69)	103	66	(66)	(98)
5	30	(39)	(32)	34	(34)	32

4. Determine the change during the period to adjust OCI to include the amount equal to the portion of the derivative increase (decrease) attributable to the lesser of the absolute value (column F)
5. Adjust the derivative to reflect its change in the fair value and adjust OCI by the amount determined by #4 above. Balance the accounting entry, if necessary, with an adjustment to earnings.

The following *financial statement effects template* walks you through the accounting for the five periods presented. Note that the account shareholder's equity is a balance sheet account that offsets the cumulative change in the fair value of the derivative. The analysis below will include gain and loss accounts in shareholder's equity. Entries to these accounts will appear on the income statement.

Financial Statement Template

Assets =	Liabilities +	Shareholder's equity (OCI)
		+ Gain on derivative – Loss on derivative

Period 1: Adjust the derivative to fair value and the OCI by the calculated amount (column F) in Measuring Hedge Effectiveness

Assets =	Liabilities +	Stockholder's equity
+ Derivative instrument + 100		+ OCI 96 + Gain on derivative + 4

Period 2: Adjust the derivative to fair value and the OCI by the calculated amount (column F) in table on Measuring Hedge Effectiveness

Assets =	Liabilities +	Stockholder's equity
+ Derivative instrument + 94		+ OCI + 98 – Loss on derivative – 4

Period 3: Adjust the derivative to fair value and the OCI by the calculated amount (column F) in table on Measuring Hedge Effectiveness

Assets =	Liabilities +	Stockholder's equity
	+ Derivative instrument + 162	− OCI − 162

Period 4: Adjust the derivative to fair value and the OCI by the calculated amount (column F) in table on Measuring Hedge Effectiveness

Assets =	Liabilities +	Stockholder's equity
	+ Derivative instrument + 101	− OCI − 98 − Loss on derivative − 3

Period 5: Adjust the derivative to fair value and the OCI by the calculated amount (column F) in table on Measuring Hedge Effectiveness

Assets =	Liabilities +	Stockholder's equity
+ Derivative instrument + 30		+ OCI + 32 − Loss on derivative − 2

Cash flow hedges, until settlement date, have their primary effect on the balance sheet. The following roll-forward schedule illustrates the impact in the shareholder's equity account OCI over the 5 periods.

Accumulated OCI (+ increases balance and − decreases balance)

Roll-Forward Schedule for Fair Value Changes in the Derivative Instrument

Period	Beginning balance	Change in fair value	Reclassification	Ending balance
1	$−	$+96	$−	$+96
2	+96	+94	+4	+194
3	+194	−162	−	+32
4	+32	−98	−	−66
5	−66	+30	−2	−34

Caution the following explanation for the changes in the balance sheet account OCI will take some time to go through. The easiest way to understand the changes is to correlate the OCI changes to *the financial statement effects template* found above.

The reclassification column relates to reclassifications between earnings and other comprehensive income. In Period 2, the +$4 in that column relates to the prior period's derivative gain that was previously recognized in earnings. That amount is reclassified to other comprehensive income in Period 2 because the cumulative gain on the derivative is less than the amount necessary to offset the cumulative change in the present value of expected future cash flows on the hedged transaction. In Period 5, the −$2 in the reclassification column relates to the derivative loss that was recognized in other comprehensive income in a prior period. At the end of Period 4, the derivative's cumulative loss of $69 was greater in absolute terms than the $66 increase in the present value of expected future cash flows on the hedged transaction. That +$3 excess had been recognized in earnings during Period 4.

In Period 5, the value of the derivative increased (and reduced the cumulative loss) by $30. The present value of the expected future cash flows on the hedged transaction decreased (and reduced the cumulative gain) by $32. The gain on the derivative in Period 5 was −$2 smaller, in absolute terms, than the decrease in the present value of the expected future cash flows on the hedged transaction. Consequently, the entire gain on the derivative is recognized in other comprehensive income. In addition, in absolute terms, the −$3 cumulative excess of the loss on the derivative over the increase in the present value of the expected future cash flows on the hedged transaction (which had previously been recognized in earnings) increased to $5. As a result, $2 is reclassified from other comprehensive income to earnings so that the $5 cumulative excess has been recognized in earnings.

The remainder of this chapter will illustrate four of the more common cash flow hedges used by companies to hedge their forecasted future cash flow needs. The four hedges are:

1. Use of an interest rate swap to hedge variable rate debt payments; this is the same example as the first illustration for fair value hedges (Chapter 3) which will enable us to compare and contrast the two hedge treatments for identical risk management strategies.

2. Use of options to hedge an anticipated purchase of inventory; this will be our first detailed look at how options are used in a company's risk management strategy.

3. Use of a commodity swap to hedge anticipated sales of crude oil; this hedge; as well as the hedge in #2, continue our emphasis on using derivative instruments on buying and selling inventory.

4. A forecasted transaction that becomes a firm commitment and then an existing asset of the company; this all in one hedge links the fair value hedge accounting for a firm commitment with the anticipated purchase of inventory (forecasted transaction) and then adds the accounting for when the firm commitment becomes an existing asset.

Cash Flow Hedge of Fixed-Rate Debt Using an Interest Rate Swap

Description of the Hedge Transaction

On June 30, 20X1, a Manufacturing Company (Company) borrows $10,000,000 of three-year 7.5% fixed-rate debt. The debt is due at maturity and contains no prepayment option. The Company, at the same time, enters into a three-year interest rate swap with a Finance Company to convert the debt's fixed rate to a variable (or floating) rate.

Under the terms of the swap, the Company receives interest at a fixed rate of 7.5% and agrees to pay interest at a variable rate equal to six-month U.S. LIBOR, based on the notional amount of $10,000,000. Both the debt and the swap require that payments be made or received on December 31 and June 30.

Note: For illustrative purposes, we will only account for the two semiannual interest periods for this interest rate swap. For an interest rate swap in which the critical terms match, accounting guidance allows companies to treat the hedge as a perfect hedge. The entries for the remaining life of the swap for the changes in the derivative instrument and the hedged item will perfectly offset in earnings.

The six-month U.S. LIBOR rate on each reset date determines the variable portion of the interest rate swap for the following six-month period. The Company designates the swap as a cash-flow hedge, which will hedge the exposure to variability in the cash flows of the variable-rate debt, with changes in cash flows that are due the changes in the six-month LIBOR the specific risk being hedged.

Hedge Documentation

a. Risk Management Strategy

The objective of entering into the hedge is to fix its cash flows associated with the risk of variability in the six-month U.S. LIBOR. In order to meet its risk management objective, the Company has decided to enter into the interest rate swap described below for the same notional amount and period of the $10,000,000 million debt entered into on June 30, X1. It is expected that this swap will fix the cash flows associated with the forecasting interest payments on the entire notional amount of the debt. The company is hedging its interest rate risk.

b. Hedging Instrument

$10,000,000 notional amount, pay fixed at 7.5% and receive variable at U.S. LIBOR, dated June 30, 20X1, with semi annual payments due on December 31, X1 and June 30, X2 and ending on June 30, 20X4.

c. Hedged Item

Forecasted interest payments on notional of $10,000,000 debt entered into on June 30, X1, and ending on June 30, X4. Reset dates for December 31, X1 and June 30, X2 determine the interest rates to be paid. These reset rates will be determined by U.S. LIBOR. The six-month U.S. LIBOR variable rate on the reset date determines the variable interest amount for the following six-month period.

d. Assessing Hedge Effectiveness

The Company has determined that the critical terms match for the derivative instrument and the hedged item and is, therefore, assuming no ineffectiveness at inception and over the term of the interest rate swap. Since there is no ineffectiveness all changes in the fair value of the interest rate swap will be recorded in OCI in the shareholder's equity.

Accounting Guidance to qualify as a perfect hedge for an interest rate swap requires that companies perform the following steps:

- Determine the difference between the variable rate to be received on the swap and the variable rate to be paid on the debt.
- Combine the difference with the fixed rate to be paid on the swap.
- Compute and recognize interest expense using the combined rate and variable-rate debt's principal amount. For the interest-rate swap hedge above, the table would be as follows in the company's determination of interest expense.

Note: For illustration purposes, we will only use the December 30, X1 and the June 30, X2 semiannual interest payment dates.

Calculation of Interest Expense

Date	(a) Difference between variable rates	(b) Fixed rate on the swap	(c) Sum (a) + (b)	(d) Principal amount of debt	(e) Semiannual interest Expense ((c) × (d))/2
12/31/X1	0.00%	7.5%	7.5%	$10 Million	$375,000
6/30/X2	0.00%	7.5%	7.5%	$10 Million	$375,000

- Determine the fair value of the interest rate swap. The table below indicates the interest rate swaps fair value for December 31, X1 and June 30, X2.

Date	Six-month U.S. LIBOR rate	Swap fair value + Asset − Liability
6/30/X1	6.00%	Zero value at inception
12/31/X1	7.00%	$+323,000 Obtained from dealer quotes
06/30/X2	5.50%	$−55,000 Obtained from dealer quotes

- The last step in the process is to adjust the carrying amount of the swap and adjust OCI by an offsetting amount.

The following accounting entries will demonstrate the financial statement impacts of a cash flow hedge on the variability of interest payments.

Assets =	Liabilities +	Stockholder's equity
		+ OCI – Interest Expense

June 30, X1

To record the issuance of debt

Assets =	Liabilities +	Stockholder's equity
+ Cash + 10,000,000	+ Debt + 10,000,000	

Note: the swap asset/liability has zero value at inception because the underlying value driver (U.S. LIBOR) has not changed

December 31, X1

To record semiannual interest on the debt a 6.00% annual percentage rate (APR):

Assets =	Liabilities +	Stockholder's equity
– Cash – 300,000		– Interest expense – 300,000

Calculation is $10,000,000 \times (6\%/2) = \$300,000$

To record settlement of the semiannual swap payment at 7.5% less the amount receivable at 6% U.S. LIBOR, as an adjustment to interest expense:

Assets =	Liabilities +	Stockholder's equity
– Cash – 75,000		– Interest expense – 75,000

Calculation is $10,000,000 \times (7.5\% - 6\%)/2 = \$75,000$

To record the change in fair value of the interest rate swap with the offset amount to OCI:

Assets =	Liabilities +	Stockholder's equity
+ Swap contract + 323,000		+ OCI + 323,000

Amount is taken from the table above and is the result from a dealer quote.

Note: For cash flow hedges, there is no income statement component (unless there is some hedge ineffectiveness) until settlement of the hedge for the derivative instrument. In the accounting entry above the asset swap contract will be offset by the change in the OCI account in shareholders equity. There is, however, an income statement effect on interest expense. The company records its variable rate payment of interest expense at 6% times the notional amount and also pays an additional $75,000 to counterparty, which is calculated as notional × (7.5% −6%)/2.

The attractiveness of a using a cash flow hedge on the variability of payments set by the benchmark rate (in this case U.S. LIBOR) is that the variable interest amounts are fixed (known with certainty) over the term of the swap.

June 30, X2

To record the interest payment to debt holders at the 7% variable rate:

Assets =	Liabilities +	Stockholder's Equity
− Cash − 350,000		− Interest expense − 350,000

Calculation is $10,000,000 × (7%/2) = $350,000

To record the payment of semiannual interest at 7.5%, less amount receivable of 7% as an adjustment to interest expense:

Assets =	Liabilities +	Stockholders Equity
− Cash − 25,000		− Interest expense − 25,000

To record change in fair value of the swap contract from dealer quote:

Assets =	Liabilities +	Stockholder's Equity
– Swap Contract – 378,000		– OCI – 378,000

Note: The derivative instrument (swap contract) will continue to be recorded at its fair value of the balance sheet over the term of the swap agreement with the offset being to OCI in shareholders equity. The change in fair value of the derivative instrument should be thought of as a gain (in the money) or as a loss (out of the money). However, the gain or loss amount is an adjustment to the OCI in shareholders equity until the hedge is settled.

In the accounting entries above for interest expense, the amounts accumulated in OCI are "indirectly" recognized as periodic settlements of the swap in interest expense at each reset date. At the end of the term of the swap, the OCI account will go to zero and the cumulative adjustments to interest expense will have been indirectly charged to earnings. It is this arbitrary accounting that can cause difficulty in determining hedge effectiveness by examining the impacts of the balance sheet. Compare this accounting to a fair value hedge where we can closely track the changes of the derivative instrument and the hedged item fair value changes on the balance sheet.

For our next comprehensive illustration, we will examine the financial statement effects of a cash flow hedge of a forecasted purchase. What makes this an interesting hedge is that we will use one commodity to hedge a different commodity.

Cash Flow Hedge of a Forecasted Purchase Using a Futures Contract

On January 1, X1, the Company, a large airline company, forecasts the purchase of 84 million gallons of jet fuel in six months. The company is concerned that jet fuel prices will rise over the coming months, so it enters into 2,000 long (purchase) contracts for purchase of 42,000 gallons per contract of heating oil futures. Each contract of heating oil is for $0.4649/gallon with settlement date on June 30, X1. We will assume that no premium was required to enter into the contracts and that any interest earned or expensed is ignored. These exceptions will allow us to focus on the hedged transaction.

The Company's risk management strategy is to hedge its exposure the price risk due to adverse changes in jet fuel prices. The Company expects some ineffectiveness in the hedged transaction because it is hedging heating oil futures contracts against the expected rise in the jet fuel prices over the term of the hedge. The Company has accepted the basis risk (changes in price between two different commodities), but still expects the hedged transaction to be highly effective.

The Company prepares the following analysis for the period ending March 31, X1, and for June 30, X1, as a basis for determining hedge effectiveness and the potential financial statement effects.

Analysis to determine fair value as of March 31, X1

Period Ending 3/31/X1	6/30/X1 Heating oil futures contracts	6/30/X1 Expected cash flows of jet fuel purchases
Futures price—end of period	$0.4726	$0.4759
Futures price—beginning of period	0.4649	0.4688
Change in price over since 1/1/X1	0.0077	0.0071
Gallons hedged under contract	84,000,000	84,000,000
Change in fair value—gain (loss)	$646,800	
Change in expected cash flows—gain (loss)		$(596,400)

Note: Using the cumulative dollar-offset method in determining hedge effectiveness, we get ($646,800/$596,400) = 108%. This amount is within the 80% to 125% and the hedge is considered highly effective.

Analysis to determine fair value as of June 30, X1

Period ending 6/30/X1	6/30/X1 Heating oil futures contracts	6/30/X1 Expected cash flow on jet fuel purchase
Spot and futures price at end of period	$0.4768	$0.4810
Futures price at beginning of period 3/31/X1	0.4726	0.4759
Change in price per gallon	0.0042	0.0051
Gallons hedged	84,000,000	84,000,000
Change in fair value—gain (loss)	$352,800	

(Continued)

Period ending 6/30/X1	6/30/X1 Heating oil futures contracts	6/30/X1 Expected cash flow on jet fuel purchase
Change in expected cash flows—gain (loss)		$(428,400)
Cumulative change in fair value/expected cash flows over the term of the hedge	$999,600	$(1,024,800)

Note: Cumulative dollar offset is ($999,600/1,024,800) = 98%

Risk Management Strategy

The objective of the hedge is to reduce the variability of the expected cash flows of the forecasted purchase of jet fuel on June 30, X1. Changes in the fair values of heating oil futures are expected to be highly effective at off-setting changes in the expected future cash flows of jet fuel due to changes in price.

Hedging Instrument

2,000 long (purchase) for June 30, X1, for heating oil futures contracts at $0.4649 per gallon. Each contract is 42,000 gallons.

Hedged Item

Forecasted purchase of 84,000,000 million gallons of jet fuel on the same date the heating oil futures contract matures on June 30, X1.

Assessing Hedge Effectiveness

Based on performing a regression analysis using past six-month periods of time the Company determined that there is a high correlation between the price of heating oil and the price of jet fuel. Based on that determination, the company concluded that the correlation will continue in the future and deemed the hedge to be highly effective as of the inception of the hedge on Jan 1, X1. On an ongoing basis in determining hedge effectiveness, the Company will use the cumulative dollar-offset method. The Company will compare the estimated cash flows on the heating oil futures contracts with the expected cash flows on the jet fuel contracts. Both the derivative instrument and the hedged item (forecasted cash flows) will be based on the forward prices. Ongoing effectiveness analysis will be updated on March 30, X1, and June 30, X1. (see above)

The following transactions will now illustrate the financial statement effects of the hedged transaction.

Financial Statement Template

Assets =	Liabilities +	+Stockholder's Equity
		+ OCI + Income from hedge ineffective – Expense for hedge ineffectiveness

Jan 1, X1
No entry required because the futures contact has zero value at inception

March 31, X2
To record the changes in fair value of the futures contracts and the change in forecasted expected cash flows.

Assets =	Liabilities +	Stockholder's Equity
+ Future contract + 646,800		+ OCI + 596,400 + Expense + 50,400

Note: The change in fair value of the futures contract is recorded as an asset based on the analysis of fair value as of March 31, X1. The offset account OCI is limited to the amount of the changes in expected future cash flows (hedged item). The remainder would be recorded as an expense due to hedge ineffectiveness.

In cash flow hedge, the amount of the "overhedge" ($646,800 – $596,400) = $50,400 is recognized in earnings normally as other expense. In the "underhedge" (in this case the change in the expected future cash flows would be greater than the change in the derivative instrument), the change in fair value of the derivative would be recognized entirely with an equal offset amount to OCI.

June 30, X1

To record the change in fair value of the futures contracts and the change in expected cash flows from purchase of jet fuel:

Assets =	Liabilities +	Stockholder's Equity
+ Futures contracts + 352,800		+ OCI + 403,200 – Expense – 50,400

Note: The asset account futures contract is now valued at $999,600 as is the OCI account. The calculation for the OCI account is ($596,400 + $403,200) = $699,600. Also, note the income and expense from hedge ineffectiveness offset each other by the settlement date.

To record the settlement of the futures contract:

Assets =	Liabilities +	Stockholder's Equity
+ Cash + 996,600 – Futures contract – 999,600		

To record the purchase of jet fuel:

Assets =	Liabilities +	Stockholder's Equity
+ Jet fuel inventory + 40,404,000 – Cash – 40,404,000		

Note: the 84,000,000 gallons of jet fuel are purchased at the spot price on June 30, X1, which is $0.4810

To record the use of the jet fuel used in the following period (entry would be made on September 30, X1):

Assets =	Liabilities +	Stockholders Equity
– Jet fuel inventory – 40,400,000		– Air fuel expense – 39,404,400 – OCI – 999,600

Note: The balance in the OCI account is written off to earnings when the company uses the inventory. The amount written off then reduces the aircraft fuel expense. Think of a credit balance in OCI as a deferred gain.

Analysis

The financial statement impact of the hedged transaction was to lock in the price of the 84,000,000 gallons of jet fuel at $0.4691 ($39,404,000/ 84,000,000) instead of the spot price of $0.4810. The hedge wasn't perfectly effective, however, resulting in ($1,024,800 –999,600) going to earnings.

The final illustration in this chapter of a cash flow hedge will be:

Accounting for a Forecasted Transaction That Becomes a Firm Commitment

On November 1, X1, a company which produces a bread-based product, determines that it needs 100,000 bushels of wheat in the last week of February, X2.

The company enters into a March 20, X2, forward contract (20,000 bushels per contract) to purchase wheat at $3.00 per bushel. The company designates the forward contracts as a hedge of forecasted cash flow purchases of inventory of 100,000 bushels of wheat on February 25, X2.

On December 31, X2, the company issues a purchase order to buy 100,000 bushels of wheat at $2.80 per bushel, to be delivered on February 25, X2. The company closes out its forward contracts purchased on November 1, X1 on February 25, 20X2.

Risk Management Strategy

The designated risk being hedged is risk of changes in cash flows relating to all the changes in the purchase price of the wheat inventory. This is cash-flow hedge of a forecasted transaction from the period November 1, X1 to December 31, X2. At that date, the company enters into a firm commitment to purchase 100,000 bushels of wheat at $2.80, which is a fair value hedge.

Hedging Instrument

On November 1, X1, the company enters into forward contracts to by 100,000 bushels of wheat at $3.00 per bushel. The company designates the forward contracts as a hedge on forecasted wheat inventory purchases on February 25, X2.

Hedged Item

From the period November 1, X1 to the period February 24, X2 the company is hedging its exposure to the variability of cash flows for the 100,000 bushels of wheat inventory needed on Feb 25, X2.

On December 31, X1, the company enters into a firm commitment to purchase 100,000 bushels of wheat at $2.80 per bushel.

After cash flow hedge accounting has been discontinued of December 31, X1, for the forecasted transaction, the forward contracts can be redesignated as fair value hedge. However, in a fair value hedge we are turning fixed cash flows into variable cash flows and the forward contract is a fixed price. The forward contracts do not represent a fair value hedge of the firm commitment. We could however get a fair value hedge on the firm commitment if we sell an equivalent number of forward contracts on wheat inventory.

Assessing Hedge Effectiveness

The company will assess hedge effectiveness based on the changes in forward prices. The company expects the forward price changes on the forward contracts to be highly effective when compared to expected future cash flows for the purchase of bushels of wheat.

Note: The forward contract can be net settled at any time because of the ready market for bushels of wheat contracts that are convertible into cash.

Changes in the fair value of the contracts during the term of the hedge(s)

	December 31, X1	February 25, X2
Forward price at beginning of period	$3.00	$2.80
Forward price at end of period	2.80	3.10
Change in price, per bushel	(0.20)	0.30
Bushels under contract	100,000	100,000
Change in fair value of contracts—gain (loss)	$20,000	$30,000

The financial statement effects and related explanations are as follows:

Assets =	Liabilities +	Stockholder's Equity
		+ OCI + Gain on hedge − Loss on hedge + Gain on forward contract − Cost of sales

November 1, X1

No entry is recorded because the forward contract has zero value at inception.

December 31, X1

To record the change in fair value of the forward contract and the offsetting entry to OCI

Assets =	Liabilities +	Stockholder's Equity
	− Forward contract − 20,000	− OCI − 20,000

Note: Forward contract is a liability with an amount of $20,000 with the same amount recorded in OCI representing a deferred loss. The amount in the OCI account will stay on the financial statements until we purchase the inventory.

Feb 24, X2

To record the change in fair value of the forward contracts:

Assets =	Liabilities +	Stockholder's Equity
+ Forward contracts + 30,000		+ Gain on forward contracts + 30,000

Note: The cash flow hedge expired on December 31, X1 and the remaining term of the forward contracts did not qualify as a hedge of the firm commitment. The forward contract is recorded as a gain to earnings.

To net settle the forward contracts:

Assets =	Liabilities +	Stockholder's Equity
+ Cash + 10,000 − Forward contracts − 10,000		

Note: The company settles the forward contracts for cash. The amount is the net of the $20,000 deferred loss in OCI and the $30,000 gain on forward contract.

To record the purchase of wheat inventory:

Assets =	Liabilities +	Stockholder's Equity
+ Wheat inventory + 280,000 – Cash – 280,000		

Note: Inventory is purchased at the firm commitment price of $2.80 per bushel X 100,000 bushels.

To record write off of OCI when the cereal products are sold:

Assets =	Liabilities +	Stockholder's Equity
		+ OCI + of sales – 20,000

CHAPTER 5

Foreign Currency Hedges

About This Chapter

Foreign currency derivatives and hedging activities continues to illustrate the previous accounting guidance for fair value and cash flows hedges for companies that conduct business in more than one currency. The accounting guidance for derivative and hedge accounting on how to account for foreign currency transactions is limited to:

- Continuing to permit hedge accounting for the type of hedge items (e.g., net investments and firm commitments) and hedging instruments (e.g., derivatives and nonderivatives) that were previously permitted under accounting guidance for foreign currency transactions and financial reporting
- Increasing the consistency of hedge accounting guidance for foreign currency hedges and other types of hedges by broadening the scope of foreign currency hedges that are eligible for hedge accounting (endnote ASC 830)

The previous illustrations on accounting for fair value and cash flow hedges will be applied to foreign currency hedges, including the hedge of a net investment in a foreign subsidiary. This chapter will focus on any differences of what derivative instruments qualify as hedges of a company's price (market) risk due to changes in exchange rates between currencies. As usual we will use comprehensive illustrations to demonstrate the accounting and documentation requirements for foreign currency hedges. Special attention will be devoted to hedging the net investment of a foreign-controlled subsidiary.

Foreign Currency Hedges

Accounting guidance permits three major exceptions to the general principles to accounting for derivative instruments and hedging activities from our previous discussions in chapter 1. These exceptions are:

1. A nonderivative financial instrument denominated in a foreign currency to be designated as a hedge of a firm commitment (fair value hedge).
2. A derivative or nonderivative financial instrument denominated in a foreign currency to be designated as a hedge of foreign currency exposure of a net investment in a foreign operation.
3. A recognized foreign-currency-denominated asset or liability for which a transaction gain or loss in recognized in earnings to be the hedged item in a fair value or cash flow hedge.

Accounting for Foreign Currency Transactions

The complexity of accounting for foreign currency transactions is that accounting standard setters, both U.S. GAAP and IFRS, had derivative and hedging guidance in place for foreign currency transactions that were not superseded by the issuance of the present accounting guidance for derivative instruments and hedging activities. This complicates the understanding of the derivative instruments, impact on financial statements by requiring adherence to two sets of reasonably complicated accounting standards. Let's proceed with an explanation of accounting for foreign currency transactions and then dive into placing a hedge around the existing asset, liability, firm commitment, or forecasted future cash flows.

A foreign currency transaction is a transaction between (for our purposes) U.S. companies and foreign suppliers or customers in which the transaction is denominated in a foreign currency measured on the financial statements in dollars ($). In essence, every foreign currency transaction is two transactions; 1) operating transaction; and 2) financing transaction. The operating transaction component is normally the buying and selling of products or services. The operating portion does not result in a gain or loss due to price risk caused by the movement of the dollar against the foreign exchange currency. There will, however, be a transaction gain or loss due to changes in the currencies that are recorded as a finance gain or loss.

Foreign currency rates are determined by comparing the price of one country's currency (U.S. dollar) with what that currency can purchase in foreign currency units (FC). The rates can be expressed *directly*—amount of currency needed to acquire one unit of foreign currency or *indirectly*—amount of foreign currency that can be acquired per unit of domestic currency. For example, at present (exchange rates change every business day) the Great Britain Pound (GBP) is trading at $1: GPB 1.50272. To determine the United States Dollar (USD) we would divide the value of the GPB into 1 USD and arrive at $0.66546. This translates to the USD is worth $0.66546 when compared to the GPB.

Currency rates of foreign countries when compared to the USD are generally floating rates. That is, based on the particular relative economic conditions for that country (or the European Union which has the Euro) their currency floats against the dollar. China is the exception as they peg their currency to be relatively constant against the dollar as a component of governmental policy. These floating exchange rates against the USD causes the financial gain or loss when companys get paid in foreign currencies (FC) for sales made or when making purchases of goods and services that occur on a date other than the operating transaction date. This is what is meant by the strengthening of the USD or the weakness of the USD when compared to FCs. For example, if the GPB goes to 1.6025 as measured against the USD, the USD equivalent would be $0.62. The dollar weakened against the GBP. This is the risk of foreign currency transactions, the FC strengthens against the dollar, making the USD less valuable or the USD rises against the FC making the FC less valuable. The management of these risks, by using derivative instruments, depends on whether the company is receiving assets (cash) or paying off liabilities.

When companies are receiving assets they would prefer that the foreign currency strengthen against the dollar. Since foreign currency (FC) business transactions are settled in the local foreign currency then remeasured to U.S. dollars, the rising FC will be worth more dollars and result in an exchange gain being recorded. When the company is paying liabilities, it wants the opposite, the USD rising against the FC. In that case, the USD buys more FCs to settle the transaction.

The accounting framework used account for import and export transactions is as follows:

1. Restate foreign currency invoice price into U.S. dollars using the appropriate foreign exchange spot rate.
2. Record an exchange gain or loss that causes the dollar amounts to differ from the original transaction.
3. If the transaction is not settled at a balance sheet reporting date (normally quarterly) record an exchange gain or loss by adjusting the receivable or payable to its dollar equivalent using the spot rate on the balance sheet reporting date.

The following examples[1] will illustrate the *accounting for foreign currency transactions*.

On October 16, X1, a Retailer purchased sweaters at an invoice price of 17,000 New Zealand dollars (NZ$) from a New Zealand manufacturer. The exchange rate was $.0.62: NZ$. Payment was due on December 16, X1.

Financial Statement Template

Assets =	Liabilities +	Stockholder's equity
		+ Exchange gain – Exchange loss

To record the purchase of sweater inventory on October 16

Assets =	Liabilities +	Stockholder's equity
+ Inventory + 10,540	+ Accounts payable + 10,540	

Note: The calculation is NZ$ 17,000 X $0.62 = $10,540. The transaction is denominated in NZ$, but measured in USD. The accounts payable will be settled in NZ$ based on their $ equivalent on the settlement date.

On December 16, the Retailer purchases 17,000 NZ$ at an exchange rate of $0.63: NZ$ and transmits to manufacturers bank in New Zealand.

Assets =	Liabilities +	Stockholder's equity
	+ Accounts payable + 710	– Exchange loss – 710

Note: Accounts payable amount is now NZ$17,000 X $0.63 = $17,710, which is $710 greater than the amount recorded on October 16.

Assets =	Liabilities +	Stockholder's equity
+ Foreign Currency + 10,710 – Cash – 710,000		

Assets =	Liabilities +	Stockholder's equity
– Foreign currency – 10,710	– Accounts payable – 10,710	

Note: The strengthening of the NZ$ against the USD and the company is a liability position caused by the foreign currency loss. Also, note that the inventory account, the operating aspect of the transaction, is not changed due to currency changes, instead the balance sheet account is changed.

The following illustration will involve accounting for a sale and making the adjustment on the balance sheet reporting date.

On November 20, X1, the Retailer sold wool coats to a Canadian company for 9,800 Canadian dollars (C$) when the spot exchange rate was $0.95: C$. Payment was due on January 20, X2. The company's fiscal year ended on December 31, X1. The exchange rate on December 31, X1, was $0.985: C$ and the exchange rate on January 20, X2 was $.995: C$.

Assets =	Liabilities +	Stockholder's equity
		+ Exchange gain – Exchange loss + Revenue

To record the sale wool coats to a Canadian company on November 20:

Assets =	Liabilities +	Shareholder's equity
+ Accounts receivable + 9,310		+ Revenue + 9,310

Calculations to derive the asset and revenue amounts recorded are 9,800C $ × $0.95 =$9,310

January 31 entry to record the appropriate adjustment on the financial statements:

Assets =	Liabilities +	Shareholder's equity
+ Accounts receivable + 343		+ Exchange gain + 343

Calculations to derive increased asset value at the reporting date are C\$ (9,800 x \$0.985) − 9,310 = \$343. The USD weakened against the C\$ leading the foreign currency buying more dollars.

On January 20, X2, the company received payment from the Canadian company at the spot rate of \$0.995, and exchanged the Canadian currency for USD, after adjustment for the movement of the C\$ against the USD.

To record changes due to a strengthened C\$:

Assets =	Liabilities +	Shareholder's equity
+ Accounts receivable + 98		+ Exchange gain + 98

To record the collection of the account receivable from the Canadian company:

Assets =	Liabilities +	Shareholder's equity
+ Foreign currency + 9,751 − Accounts receivable − 9,751		

To record the exchange of C\$ to USD:

Assets =	Liabilities +	Shareholder's equity
+ Cash + 9,751 − Foreign currency − 9,751		

Note: The foreign currency strengthened against the USD, resulting in the foreign currency buying more dollars.

The illustrations above demonstrate the exchange (price) risk that companies have to take when selling and purchasing products and services in international markets. The company challenge in managing the price risk is two-fold: (a) Will the USD rise or fall against the particular foreign currency in which the company has economic transactions? and (b) Is the company in a net asset position or a net liability position with regard to its current operations? The combination of the company's perspective of the answers to the two questions above will determine its risk management strategy. Derivative instruments that can be used as hedges of the financial risk (each foreign currency transaction has an operating and financial risk) can be a very effective way for companies to manage those risks. The following simplified example will illustrate the accounting for a hedge of exposed assets using a forwards sale contract.

The Retailer sold goods for 2,000 GBP to a British customer on Oct 1, X1, when the spot rate was $2.10: GBP. Payment in pounds is due on March 1, X2. On the same date as the operating transaction was entered into, Retailer enters into a forward sale contract to deliver 2,000 GBP on March 1, X2, at a forward rate of $2.11/GBP.

Assets =	Liabilities +	Stockholder's equity
		+ Revenue + Exchange gain – Exchange loss

Retailer records the sale of goods to the British Customer on October 1:

Assets =	Liabilities +	Shareholder's equity
+ Accounts receivable + 4,200		+ Revenue + 4,200

Calculation to record revenue is $2.10 \times 2,000 = \$4,200$

Note: No entry is required for the forward contract since its fair value is zero because the contract price and the forward price are the same at contract inception. When the forward price moves over the life of the hedge, then a gain or loss will be recorded.

Retailer records a year-end adjustment for both the changes in the spot rate (financial component of the sales transaction) and an adjustment for the changes in the forward rate on the derivative instrument. On December 31, X1, the spot rate for GBP has moved to $2.15/GBP and the forward rate for delivery is now $2.16/GBP.

To record the changing value of exchange spot rates on the financial statements:

Assets =	Liabilities +	Shareholder's equity
+ Accounts receivables + 100		+ Exchange gain + 100

Calculation is ($2.15 − $2.10) × 2,000 = $100

To record the change in fair value of the forward contract:

Assets =	Liabilities +	Shareholder's equity
	+ Forward contract + 100	− Exchange loss − 100

Calculation is ($2.16 − $2.11) × 2,000 = 100

On March 1, X2, the British customer pays the Retailer and the company settles the forward contract. The spot rate and the forward rate have converged to $2.18/GBP.

To record the changing value of the exchange spot rates on the financial statements:

Assets =	Liabilities +	Shareholder's equity
+ Accounts receivable + 60		+ Exchange gain + 60

Calculation is ($2.18 − $2.15) × 2,000 = $60

To record the changing fair value of the derivative instrument:

Assets =	Liabilities +	Shareholder's equity
	+ Forward contract + 40	− Exchange loss − 40

Assets =	Liabilities +	Shareholder's equity
		– Exchange loss – 40

Calculation is ($2.18 – $2.16) × 2,000 = $40

To record payment to the British customer on March 1, X2:

Assets =	Liabilities +	Shareholder's equity
+ Foreign currency + 4,360 – Accounts receivable – 4,360		

Calculation is $4,200 + $100 +$60 = $4,360

To record the delivery of the foreign currency and settlement of the forward contract on March 1, X1:

Assets =	Liabilities +	Shareholder's equity
+ Cash + 4,220 – Foreign c urrency – 4,360	– Forward contract – 140	

Analysis: the company receives foreign currency (GBP) based on the forward contract of 2,000 × $2.11 = $4,220 and closed out the forward contract liability account and the foreign currency account.

The remainder of this chapter will demonstrate through comprehensive illustrations the most popular foreign currency hedges used by companies.[2]

Use of a Forward Exchange Contract to Hedge a Firm Commitment to Pay Foreign Currency

A U.S. company enters into a firm commitment with a foreign supplier on September 30, X1, to purchase equipment for foreign currency (FC) 10,000,000. The equipment is deliverable on March 31, X2, and is payable on June 30, X2. In order to hedge the commitment to pay foreign currency of 10,000,000, the company enters into a forward exchange contract on September 30, X1, to receive FC 10,000,000 on June 30, X2 at an exchange rate of FC1=U.S.$0.72.

The company assesses hedge effectiveness based on the measurement of the difference between changes in the value of the forward exchange contract and the USD equivalent of the firm commitment. Since both of the fair value changes are calculated based on changes in the forward rates from inception to June 30, X2, the company determines there will be no hedge ineffectiveness.

Foreign Currency (FC)/U.S. Exchange Rates

Date	Spot rates	Forward rates for June 30, X2
September 30,X1	FC 1 = $0.65	FC 1 = $0.72
December 31, X1	FC 1 = $0.66	FC 1 = $0.71
March 31, X2	FC 1 = $0.69	FC 1 = $0.71
June 30, X2	FC 1 = $0.70	Spot and forward rates converge

As the basis for determining the impact on the financial statements over the term of the hedging relationship the company prepares the following fair value analysis assuming zero hedge ineffectiveness. The fair value analysis is based on changes in the forward rates for both the derivative instrument (forward contract) and the firm commitment discounted at 6.00% to determine the net present value.

Date	Fair value of forward contract discounted at 6.00%	Change in fair value of forward contract gain (loss)
September 30, X1	$–	$–
December 31, X1	(97,066)*	(97,066)
March 31, X2	(98,522)**	(1,456)
June 30, X2	(200,000)***	(101,478)
Total		($200,000)

*[FC 10,000,000 × (0.71 −0.72)/[1.06/4)]^2 = (97,066)
**[FC 10,000,000 × (0.71 −0.72)]/1.06/4 = 98,522
***[FC 10,000,000 × (0.70 −0.72)] = 200,000

Hedge Documentation

a. Risk Management Strategy

The objective of the transaction is to hedge the changes in the fair value of the equipment purchase (fair value hedge) firm commitment attributable to changes in foreign currency forward rates between the foreign currency (FC) and the USD. The company entered into a forward contract to purchase FC 10,000,000 on September 30, XI, to receive FC 10,000,000 on June 30, X2 to reduce the risk in the variability of foreign currency exchange rates.

b. Hedging Instrument

A forward contract to buy FC 10,000,000 at an exchange rate of FC 1 = U. S. $0.72 on June 30, X2.

c. Hedged Item

The firm commitment to purchase equipment from foreign supplier at foreign currency 10,000,000 on March 30, X2.

d. Assessing Hedge Effectiveness

The company has performed a critical terms assessment of the derivative instrument and the hedged item and concluded that the changes in fair value attributable to the changes in foreign currency and the USD are expected to be completely offset by the forward contract. The company will perform ongoing effectiveness tests by verifying and documenting that the critical terms of the firm commitment and the forward contract (derivative instrument) match.

The company documented that the critical terms match was as follows.

- The critical terms of the forward and the hedged transaction (firm commitment) are identical; same notional, same date, and same currency.
- The fair value of the forward contract at inception is zero. No amounts were paid or received and were entered into at market rates.
- Effectiveness will be based on changes in the forward rate. (ASC 815-20-25-84 (a) (b) (c))

The following illustrates the financial statement impact over the term of the derivative instrument as well as the firm commitment.

Assets =	Liabilities +	Shareholder's equity
		+ Foreign exchange gain − Foreign exchange loss

September 30, X1
No impact on financial statements as the forward contract has zero value at inception

December 31,X1
To record the change in fair value of the forward exchange contract

Assets =	Liabilities +	Stockholder's equity
	+ Forward contract payable + 97,066	− Foreign exchange loss − 97,066

Note: fair value changes are taken from the fair value table above.

To record change in the fair value of the firm commitment that is due to changes in the exchange rate:

Assets =	Liabilities +	Stockholder's Equity
+ Firm commitment + 97,066		+ Foreign exchange gain + 97,066

Note: for a fair value hedge if the derivative instrument (forward contract) goes out of the money then the accounting rules require that the firm commitment offset the liability recorded that is equal to the loss on foreign exchange, be offset by a gain on foreign exchange with the offset being to an asset account firm commitment.

March 31, X2
To record the change in fair value of the forward exchange contract

Assets =	Liabilities +	Stockholder's Equity
	+ Forward contract payable + 1,456	− Foreign exchange loss − 1,456

Note: the amount recorded on March 31 increase the balance sheet account forward contract payable to $98,522

To record the change in fair value of the firm commitment due to changes in foreign exchange rates:

Assets =	Liabilities +	Stockholder's Equity
+ Firm commitment + 1,456		+ Foreign exchange gain + 1,456

Note: the amount recorded on March 31 for the asset account firm commitment will now be equal to the account balance for the forward contract payable.

To record receipt of the equipment on March 31, X2 at the forward contract rate established by the hedging transaction:

Assets =	Liabilities +	Stockholder's Equity
+ Equipment + 6,998,522 – Firm commitment – 98,522	+ Equipment payable + 6,900,000	

Note: the equipment is recorded at the spot price on March 31, X2, of $0.69 × FC 10,000,000 = $6,900,000. The firm commitment asset is written off at its carrying value of $98,522. The equipment then is recorded at the combination of the two amounts. Also, note that the equipment will not be placed in service until the payment date of June 30, X2, so no depreciation would be recorded on June 30, X2.

June 30, X2

To recognize the change in fair value of the forward contract:

Assets =	Liabilities +	Stockholder's Equity
	+ Forward contract payable +101,478	– Foreign exchange loss – 101,478

Note: The company has a natural hedge on the derivative instrument since it settled the firm commitment hedge transaction on March 31, X2. The foreign-currency-denominated payable is remeasured to the company's reporting currency (USD) using the reporting period and changes in the spot rate. For the remainder of the transaction (converting FC to cash to pay the account payable) the change in fair value of the forward contract consists of these components:

1. Change in the spot rate
2. Interest on opening fair value
3. Change is spot/forward differential

This will cause some recorded income statement mismatch in the forward contract the accounts payable owned due to the implicit interest cost of the forward. In the journal entry above, I assumed $98, 522 \times (6.00\%/ 4) = \$1,478$.

To recognize the transaction loss on the foreign currency account payable:

Assets =	Liabilities +	Stockholder's Equity
	+ Accounts payable + 100,000	– Foreign exchange loss – 100,000

Note: the change in the fair value of accounts payable is based solely on the changes in spot rates. FC 10,000,000 × ($0.69 – $0.70) = $100,000

To record settlement of the forward contract and the accounts payable:

Assets =	Liabilities +	Stockholder's Equity
– Cash – 7,200,000	– Forward contract payable – 200,000 – Accounts payable – 7,000,000	

Note: Settlement of the forward contract at FC 10,000,000 × $0.72 = $7,200,000. Accounts payable is FC 10,000,000 × $0.70 (spot price) = $7,000,000. The forward contract payable is written off when the derivative instrument is settled.

Analysis of the Hedged Transaction

The firm commitment was recorded $6,998,522, which consisted of the accounts payable at the spot price of $0.69 × FC 10,000,000 plus the fair value of the firm commitment. If the company which was very close to the accounts payable of $7,000,000 that was recorded. In addition, gains and losses on the firm commitment were offset, with just a small amount of earnings mismatch when we settled the forward contract. However, the movement of forward rates caused a $200,000 loss on the derivative instrument.

For the next illustration, let's examine a cash flow using foreign-currency option.

Use of Foreign-Currency Options to Hedge Forecasted Foreign Sales

Company is a U.S. reporting company with sales to foreign customers. The company's sales are denominated in foreign currencies (FC) but do not meet the accounting guidance for classification as a firm commitment. The company forecasts that as of September 30, X1, foreign currency sales of FC 10,000,000 will occur in 6 months on March 31, X2. The company has historical experience with its customers that the sales are probable of occurring. The company's risk management policy uses foreign currency put options to hedge the exchange (price) risk when selling to foreign customers. Because this is a hedge of a forecasted transaction, the company will designate as a cash flow hedge of forecasted sales.

The contractual terms and conditions of the foreign currency put are as follows:

Contract items	Put option contract terms
Contract amount	FC 10,000,000
Trade date	September 30, X1
Expiration date	March 31, X2
Foreign currency exercise rate (price)	FC 1 = $0.50
Spot rate	FC 1 = $0.50
Premium	$20,000

The premium paid for the option represents the time value only. Option premiums generally represent the time value only when purchased because the interaction between the foreign currency exercise rate of FC 1 = $0.50 and the spot rate of FC 1 = $0.50 has not moved. The difference in the spot rate from September 30, X1 and March 31, X2 will put the option in the money (spot rate rises above the exercise rate) or out of the money (spot rate falls below the exercise rate). This movement between the two rates is called the intrinsic value of the option. The foreign-currency put option is designated as hedge of the company's forecasted cash flows, and the company expects the hedge to be perfectly effective because the critical terms of the derivative instrument match the hedged item (forecasted future cash flows from sales). The company will assess hedge effectiveness at inception and over the life of the hedge on the basis of changes in the options intrinsic value—amount of positive value for the difference between the option's spot exchange rate and the exercise exchange rate. Changes in the time value (premium of $20,000) will not be hedged and will instead be written off to earnings over the term of the contract.

Risk Management Strategy

The objective of the hedged transaction is to eliminate the currency (price) risk associated with the forecasted foreign-currency denominated sales for the company which is a USD reporting currency due to changes in the FC:USD exchange rate. The derivative instrument purchase takes place on September 30, X1.

Hedging Instrument
This is a cash flow hedge in which the hedging instrument is a purchased put option to sell FC 10,000,000 with an exercise price of FC 1: $0.50 USD. The risk exposure being hedged is the variability of the future expected cash flows attributable to a specific change is exchange rates.

Hedged Item
The foreign exchange put option is designated as a foreign currency cash flow hedge of FC 10,000,000 of forecasted foreign currency sales on March 31, X2. The company has determined that the forecasted transaction is probable of occurring based on historical transactions of a similar nature and will update this assessment for each reporting period of the hedged transaction.

Assessing Hedge Effectiveness
The company assessed the critical terms of the derivative instrument and the hedged item (forecasted cash flows) and found a match such that

changes in the put options intrinsic value will completely offset the changes in the forecasted cash flows based on changes in the spot rate. The company used the following accounting guidance in determining whether the critical terms of the derivative instrument and the hedged item matched in concluding hedging effectiveness.

- The critical terms of the hedged item and the option are identical as notional, cash flow date, and currency.
- The option was at the money at inception of the hedged transaction.
- Effectiveness will be assessed based on the intrinsic value of the option. The change in the option's intrinsic value will completely offset the change in the expected cash flows based on changes in the spot rate.

The company will assess the critical terms of the hedged transaction to determine if there are any changes that would cause some ineffectiveness. The company will record in other comprehensive income (OCI) changes in the derivative instrument that are effective in offsetting changes in the forecasted cash flows due to changes in the spot rate over the term of the hedged transaction. Any change in the critical terms that cause hedging ineffectiveness between the derivative instrument and the hedged transaction will be recorded in earnings.

Prior to recording the financial statement effects of the hedged transaction, we will examine the valuation of the derivative instrument (put option) over the term of the hedged transaction.

Valuation of the Derivative Instrument

FC/U.S. $ March Contract	9/30/X1	12/31/X1	3/31/X2
Contract rate	2.00	2.00	2.00
Spot rate	2.00	2.10	2.30

Given the information above, we then perform a fair value analysis that will become the basis for recording the financial statement effects and determining hedge effectiveness.

Fair Value Analysis of Derivative Instrument

Date	Time Value	Intrinsic Value	Total Value
9/30/X1	$20,000	$—	$20,000
12/31/X1	9,000	238,095[1]	247,095
3/31/X1	——	652,174[2]	652,174

(FC 10,000,000/2.00 = $5,000,000) less (FC 10,000,000/2.10) = $4,761,905 which equals $238,095.

Taking the same $5,000,000 contract rate, we subtract the sport rate of (FC 10,000,000/2.30 = $4,347,826) = $414,079. This is the amount of the increase in intrinsic value for the March 31, X2 reporting period. In the table above, the $414,079 is added to the $238,095 to produce the reported asset value of $652,174.

Note that the time value goes to zero on settlement date. The decreasing value in time value component of the put option will go directly to earnings. However, since we are hedging the forecasted cash flows with the changes in spot rates (intrinsic value) of the derivative instrument, this produces no hedge ineffectiveness.

The following transaction history is an analysis of the financial statement effects of the hedged transaction.

Assets =	Liabilities +	Stockholder's Equity
		– Loss on hedge + OCI—deferred gain – OCI –deferred loss + Revenue

September 30, X1

To record the foreign currency option at the premium paid:

Assets =	Liabilities +	Stockholder's Equity
+ Foreign currency option + 20,000 – Cash – 20,000		

Note: The option is recorded as an asset when paid and represents the time value of option. Over the term of the hedged transaction, the time value will converge to zero, so we will write this amount off against earnings over the term of the hedged transaction.

December 31, X1

To record the change in time value of the foreign currency option;

Assets =	Liabilities +	Stockholder's Equity
– Foreign currency option – 11,000		– Loss on hedge – 11.000

Note: The computation of the time value decrease is a present value calculation using the risk-free rate and the time remaining on the option. For our purposes, they are given values.

To record the change in the intrinsic value of the option;

Assets =	Liabilities +	Stockholder's Equity
+ Foreign currency option + 238,095		+ OCI + 238,095

Note: The option goes in the money and is recorded as a deferred gain in OCI in Shareholder's equity.

March 31, X2

To record the change in the time value of the option:

Assets =	Liabilities +	Stockholder's Equity
– Foreign currency option – 9,000		– Loss on Hedge – 9,000

Note: Time value goes to zero on settlement so we remove the remaining value from the asset account foreign currency option.

To record the change in the intrinsic value of the option:

Assets =	Liabilities +	Stockholder's Equity
+ Foreign currency option + 414,079		+ OCI + 414,079

Note: Record the increase in the foreign currency option account to reflect changes in the spot rate from 2.10 to 2.30 on March 31, X2.

To record FC 10,000,000 in sales at the current spot rate of 2.30 FC/U.S.$:

Assets =	Liabilities +	Stockholder's Equity
	+ Cash + 4,347,826	+ Revenue + 4,347,826

Note: The company records the sales of FC 10,000,000 and records the U.S. dollar equivalent in revenue.

To record settlement of the derivative instrument (put option):

Assets =	Liabilities +	Stockholder's Equity
+ Cash + 652,174 + Foreign currency option + 652,174		

Note: The company settles the foreign currency option and receives cash equivalent to its intrinsic value, which is the result of the spot rates moving from 2.00 to 2.30 over the term of the hedged transaction of FC 10,000,000 as compared to the contract rate of 2.00.

To transfer the deferred gains in OCI to earnings:

Assets =	Liabilities +	Stockholder's Equity
		– OCI – 652,174 + Revenue + 652,174

Note: The hedge was done to assure that the company received at least $5,000,000 from its FC 10,000,000 sales. The transaction above when we cashed out the derivative instrument for $652,174 combined with the spot sales of $4,347,826 accomplishes our objective. The cost of the option contract of $20,000 was the cost of predictability that assured the company of revenue of $5,000,000.

The next two illustrations both involve hedging the net investment in a foreign subsidiary. Subsidiary will be used to describe the relationship when a U.S Company controls the operating and financial policies of a foreign company. The first illustration will use a forward exchange contract and the second illustration will use a non derivative contract to hedge the net investment in a foreign subsidiary. The use of a non-derivative contract in a hedged transaction is one of the exceptions to accounting guidance for hedging activities that is allowed under accounting guidance for foreign operations.

Prior to illustrating a hedge of the net investment in a subsidiary some accounting background is necessary to understand why a company would do the hedged transaction. The risk management strategy for this type of hedge is to protect the net carrying value (assets minus liabilities) of the subsidiary from adverse changes in the local foreign currency that the subsidiary uses during the year to record and report its changes in assets and liabilities. The adverse effect of foreign exchange rates is magnified by the accounting guidance that generally requires assets and liabilities to translated by the U.S. company at the spot rate for the foreign exchange equivalent using the fiscal reporting date at the end of the year.

This arbitrary accounting rule mandates that companys generally use the spot exchange rates of Foreign Currency (FC) USD in the year-end reporting date. However, during the operating year the company has been reporting changes based on exchange rates that were in effect when the transactions were originated and settled. Since exchange rates fluctuate every business day, the translation of foreign controlled companies, balance sheets and income statements to be combined with the U.S. company would never equal and would the accounting equation would be out of balance.

Accounting guidance then rectifies this imbalance by requiring the offset amount needed to balance the combined financial statements by using an account called cumulative translation adjustment (CTA) in shareholder's equity. For example, if the CTA amount needed to balance the financial statements is a credit (think gain) then the amount is added to shareholder's equity. If the amount needed to balance the financial statements is a debit (think loss) the CTA is reduced by that amount. The CTA account is a permanent balance sheet account that is carried on the financial statements of the U.S. company until they would divest the foreign subsidiary or sell a large enough interest in the subsidiary that the U.S. company would no longer control the foreign subsidiary.

The risk management strategy is to protect against a large debit CTA (loss from foreign exchange translation) because of the adverse effect on the company's shareholder equity amount as reported in the combined financial statements. Changes in shareholder equity from one balance sheet date to the next are generally viewed by financial statement users as the amount of earnings retained by the company from its earned income. The amount retained for the current year is net income earned minus the dividends paid. When companies are required by accounting rules to add in other components of shareholder equity the financial analysis of the company can be difficult to assess.

In the previous chapter on accounting for cash flow hedges, the use of the offset account other comprehensive income (OCI) can make this the analysis of changes in assets and liabilities from one year to the next or over time more difficult. In my view, that is why I look at changes to OCI over the term of the hedge as deferred gains or losses. That view does not hold for the cumulative translation adjustment because it is a purely arbitrary rule that allows combined financial statements to be in balance. They are not deferred gains and losses because normally the company has no intention of realizing the CTA amounts by immediate sale of the operating subsidiary. The way to mitigate the adverse changes or to smooth out changes to the reported amount of a foreign subsidiary on the U.S. company's financial statements is to engage in hedges of the net investment (assets minus liabilities). Since assets minus liabilities is equal to shareholder equity you are hedging the adverse change in arbitrary changes to shareholder equity not due to income earned and dividends paid.

Use of a Forward-Exchange Contract to Hedge a Net Investment in a Foreign Subsidiary

A U.S. Company has a net investment of FC 50,000,000 in a foreign subsidiary. On October 1, X1, the company enters into a six-month forward contract to sell FC 50,000,000 at FC 1 = $1.70, when the spot rate is FC 1 = $1.72 to hedge its entire net investment in foreign subsidiary of FC 50,000,000 as of the beginning of the reporting year.

The company will measure effectiveness based on the changes in the forward rates and on the beginning balance of the net investment in foreign subsidiary at the beginning of the hedging period. This will allow the company to record all changes in the fair value of the derivative instrument (forward contract) to be reported in the cumulative translation adjustment (CTA) account in shareholder's equity. The company documents that the notional of the forward contract and the hedged item match and the currency of the forward matches the currency of the foreign subsidiary.

Exchange Rates

Date	Spot	Forward
October 1, X1	FC 1 = $1.72	FC 1 = $1.70
December 31, X1	FC 1 = $1.65	FC 1 = $1.63
March 31, X2	FC 1 = $1.60	FC 1 = $1.60

We can take the hypothesized changes in exchange rates and construct our fair value analysis of the derivative instrument and the hedged item.

Fair Value Analysis of Derivative Instrument and Hedged Item

Date	Change in fair value of forward contract (discount rate used is 8%)	Change in fair value of net investment due to changes in the spot rate ( ) represents liability
October 1, X1	$—	$—
December 31, X1	3,431,373[1]	(3,500,000)[3]
March 31, X2	1,586,627	(2,500,000)
Cumulative	$5,000,000[2]	($6,000,000)[4]

[1] Fair value change on December 31, X1, is calculated as [FC 50,000,000 X (1.70 – 1.63)] /[1 +(.08/4)] = $3,431,627. Note: the change in the derivative instrument is calculated using the change in forward rates.

[2] The $5,000,000 is derived from the calculation FC 50,000,000 X (1.70 – 1.60). The change in fair value for March 31, X2, is the difference between the cumulative total and the December 31, X1, change in fair value.

[3] The $3,500,000 is derived from the calculation FC 50,000,000 X (1.72 – 1.65). Note the changes in the net investment account are computed using the changes in the spot rate, and with no discount attached.

[4] The $6,000,000 is derived from the calculation FC 50,000,000 X (1.72 – 1.60). The $2,500,000 fair value change is the difference between the cumulative change in fair and the change in fair value of the hedged item on December 31, X1.

Hedge Documentation

Risk Management Strategy

The objective of the hedged transaction is to hedge the net investment in foreign subsidiary of the company, against adverse changes in exchange rates. The Company uses the USD for reporting while the foreign subsidiary uses FC in their financial reporting. The hedge is to protect the net investment (Shareholder's equity) from movements of the FC when translated into the reporting currency U.S. dollar.

Hedging Instrument

Company will use a forward contract to sell FC 50,000,000 at FC 1 = U.S. $ 1.70. The derivative instrument is entered into on October 1, X1, and will be settled on March 31, X2.

Hedged Item

The foreign forward exchange contract is designated as a hedge of the net investment of the foreign subsidiary's beginning balance of FC 50,000,000 on October 1, X2.

Assessing Hedge Effectiveness

Hedge effectiveness will be assessed at the inception of the hedged term and over the term of the hedged transaction. Effectiveness will be based on overall changes in the fair value of the foreign forward contract. The fair value changes will be based on changes in the forward rate. The critical terms of the hedged transaction including notional, currency, and underlying for the forward contract match the same critical terms of the net investment in foreign subsidiary as of October 1, X1. As a result, the company expects the hedge to be highly effective.

The company will measure effectiveness of the forward contract on the foreign exchange risk of the net investment in subsidiary by using a hypothetical derivative. The changes in the value of the foreign forward contract will be compared to changes in the hypothetic derivative, which will be changes in the net investment in foreign subsidiary over the term of the hedge. The net investment in foreign subsidiary will be hypothetically calculated beginning at October 1, X1, and on required reporting and settlement dates over the term of the hedged transaction. The hypothetical derivatives (net investment in foreign subsidiary) changes in fair value will use the spot rates in effect over the term of the hedged transaction.

The following transaction history of the hedged transaction will demonstrate the financial statement effects.

Assets =	Liabilities +	Stockholder's Equity
		+Cumulative Translation Adjustment (CTA)

October 1, X1

No entry at inception since the FC forward equals the contract rate

December 31, X1

To record the change in fair value of the forward contract from October 1, X1 as a CTA:

Assets =	Liabilities +	Stockholder's Equity
+ Forward contract receivable + 3,431,473		+ CTA + 3,431,473

Note: the forward contract receivable goes in the money because the forward rate for the October contract for March settlement decreases on December 31, X1. The offset entry is to increase shareholder equity by increasing the cumulative translation adjustment account for the same amount.

To record the change in the foreign subsidiaries assets and liabilities (net investment in foreign subsidiary) based on changes in the spot rate from October 1, X1 to December 31, X1:

Assets =	Liabilities +	Stockholder's Equity
– Net investment in foreign subsidiary – 3,500,000		– CTA – 3,500,000

Note: The net investment decrease is calculated as per the table above based on changes in the spot rates from October 1, X1, to December 31, X1. The offset entry to CTA will represent some ineffectiveness due to the derivative instrument using the forward rate to record fair value changes and the hypothetical derivative net investment in foreign subsidiary is using the spot rate. The net investment in foreign subsidiary is carried on the controlling company's books as a single-line item in their financial statements.

March 31, X2

To record the change in the fair value of the forward contract from December 31, X2, to the settlement date:

Assets =	Liabilities +	Stockholders Equity
+ Forward contract receivable + 1,586,627		+ CTA + 1,586,627

Note: Change in the fair value on the forward contract from inception to the settlement date is $5,000,000.

To record the cash settlement of the forward contract:

Assets =	Liabilities +	Stockholder's Equity
+ Cash + 5,000,000 -Forward contract Receivable - 5,000,000		

Note: The forward contract is turned into cash on the settlement date. The $5,000,000 represents the gain from entering into the forward contract on October 1, X1.

To record the cumulative translation adjustment:

Assets =	Liabilities +	Stockholder's Equity
-Net Investment in foreign subsidiary -2,500,000		-CTA -2,500,000

Note: The forward contract went in the money by $5,000,000 while the net investment went out of the money by $6,000,000. However, for these types of hedges there is no ineffectiveness that goes to earnings. From the analysis above, note that all the adjustments are made on the balance sheet accounts of the controlling company. What appears to be ineffectiveness will not be recorded over the term of the hedged transaction.

Analysis

The controlling company will increase cash by $5,000,000 by settling the forward contract. The company will also maintain the cumulative translation adjustment account, which results in a net change of minus $1,000,000 over the term of the hedged transactions and also carry the net investment in foreign subsidiary account at $6,000,000 less than its beginning balance of FC 50,000,000, which would be carried on the company's books at FC 50,000,000 × 1.72 (spot rate) = $86,000,000.

The mathematical result of the hedged transaction was to record debits for the asset cash (forward contract receivable) and a debit net change of $1,000,000 in the cumulative translation adjustment account, which equals $6,000,000. This amount is offset by the decrease in the net investment in subsidiary account of $6,000,000, which would be the credit change in the account. The total changes when translating the FC into USD for the March 31, X2 reporting date would offset to zero. No ineffectiveness in the hedge.

CHAPTER 6

Presentation and Disclosure

About This Chapter

Disclosure and presentation requirements for companies that use derivative instruments as part of their risk management strategy are an important part of their financial reporting requirement. This chapter will present qualitative and quantitative disclosures as well as the required disclosures for fair value and cash flow hedges and the hedge of a net investment in foreign subsidiaries. In addition, the chapter will include detailed disclosure notes for the company's significant accounting policies for derivative instruments and hedging activities for all entities and for industrial/commercial entities.

Accounting guidance for derivatives disclosures makes disclosures about the fair value of financial instruments optional for entities that meet all of the following criteria.[1]

1. The company is a non-public entity
2. The company's total net assets (asset minus liabilities) are less than $100 million on the date of the financial statements
3. The company has no instrument that, in whole or in part, is accounted for as a freestanding derivative.

Disclosure objectives for derivative instruments and hedging activities are designed to assist financial statement users in understanding how derivatives are used as a part of the company's risk management strategy. These objectives are to help the users of the company's financial statements to:[1]

1. How and why a company uses derivative instruments
2. How derivative instruments and related hedging activities are accounted for

3. And, how derivative instruments and related hedging activities affect the company's financial position (balance sheet), financial performance (income statement), and cash flows (statement of cash flows).

Qualitative and Quantitative Disclosures

As described in accounting guidance, an entity that holds or issues derivative instruments (or nonderivative instruments that are designated and qualify as hedging instruments pursuant to the standards) shall disclose, for every annual and interim reporting period where a balance sheet and income statement are presented, a description of the objective, context, and strategies for issuing or holding derivatives. The purpose of these disclosures is to enhance the overall transparency of an entity's derivative transactions by helping investors and creditors understand what an entity is trying to accomplish with its derivatives.

As discussed in accounting guidance for derivative disclosures, these qualitative disclosures may be more meaningful if described in the context of an entity's overall risk-management profile. The qualitative disclosures require an entity to: (a) distinguish between objectives and strategies for derivative instruments used for risk management purposes and those used for other purposes (at a minimum based on the instruments primary underlying risk exposure such as interest rate risk, credit risk, etc.), and (b) distinguish between the accounting designations of derivative instruments (e.g., cash flow hedging, fair value hedging, and net investment hedging relationships). For derivative instruments not designated as hedging instruments, a description of the purpose of the derivative activity is also required.

An entity that holds or issues derivative instruments (or nonderivative instruments that are designated and qualify as hedging instruments pursuant to the standards) shall disclose the following, for every annual and interim reporting period, where a balance sheet and income statement are presented:

a. The location and fair value amount of derivative instruments and non-derivative instruments that are designated and qualify as hedging instruments pursuant to recommended accounting guidance.[2]

1. Present fair value on a gross basis (i.e., not giving effect to netting arrangements or collateral)
2. Segregate assets from liabilities and (a) segregate derivative instruments that are qualifying and designated as hedging instruments from those that are not; within those two categories, segregate by type of contract, and (b) disclose the line item(s) on the balance sheet in which the fair value amounts are included

Disclosure Requirements for Fair Value Hedges[3]

b. The location and amount of gains and losses related to the following:
   1. Derivative instruments qualifying and designated as hedging instruments in fair value hedges (tabular format required)
   2. Related hedged items qualifying and designated in fair value hedges
c. For derivative instruments, as well as nonderivative instruments that may give rise to foreign currency transaction gains or losses under accounting guidance for foreign currency transactions, which have been designated and have qualified as fair value hedging instruments, and for the related hedged items, an entity shall disclose:
   1. The net gain or loss recognized in earnings during the reporting period representing: (a) the amount of the hedges' ineffectiveness and (b) the component of the derivative instruments' gain or loss, if any, excluded from the assessment of hedge effectiveness.
   2. The amount of net gain or loss recognized in earnings when a hedged firm commitment no longer qualifies as a fair value hedge.
   Disclosure requirements for cash flow hedges:
d. The location and amount of gains and losses by the type of contract related to:
   1. The effective portion recognized in other comprehensive income (tabular format required)
   2. The effective portion subsequently reclassified to earnings (tabular format required)
   3. The ineffective portion and the amount excluded from effectiveness testing (tabular format required)

e. A description of the transactions or other events that will result in the reclassification into earnings of gains and losses that are reported in accumulated other comprehensive income.

f. The estimated net amount of the existing gains or losses at the reporting date that is expected to be reclassified into earnings within the next 12 months.

g. The maximum length of time over which the entity is hedging its exposure to the variability in future cash flows for forecasted transactions excluding those forecasted transactions related to the payment of variable interest on existing financial instruments.

h. The amount of gains and losses reclassified into earnings as a result of the discontinuance of cash flow hedges because it is probable that the original forecasted transactions will not occur by the end of the originally specified time period or within the additional period of time discussed in the standard.

Disclosure Requirements for Net Investment Hedges

Location and amount of gains and losses by type of contract are related to the following:

1. The effective portion recognized in other comprehensive income (tabular format required)
2. The effective portion subsequently reclassified to earnings (tabular format required)
3. The ineffective portion and the amount excluded from effectiveness testing (tabular format required)

The following two comprehensive disclosure examples are presented in two parts. In the first part is an example of a generic disclosure note for all companies using derivative instruments for hedging activities.[4] The second qualitative disclosure note will be the required additional exposures for commercial or industrial companies.

Qualitative Disclosures for Derivatives Instruments and Hedging Activities

1. All derivatives are recognized on the balance sheet at their fair value. On the date that the Company enters into a derivative contract, it designates

the derivative as: (1) a hedge of (a) the fair value of a recognized asset or liability or (b) an unrecognized firm commitment (a fair value hedge), (2) a hedge of (a) a forecasted transaction or (b) the variability of cash flows that are to be received or paid in connection with a recognized asset or liability (a cash flow hedge), (3) a foreign-currency fair value or cash flow hedge (a foreign currency hedge), (4) a hedge of a net investment in a foreign operation, or (5) an instrument that is held for trading or nonhedging purposes (a "trading" or "nonhedging" instrument).

Changes in the fair value of a derivative that is highly effective and that is designated and qualifies as a fair value hedge, along with changes in the fair value of the hedged asset or liability that are attributable to the hedged risk (including changes that reflect losses or gains on firm commitments), are recorded in current-period earnings. Changes in the fair value of a derivative that is highly effective as and that is designated and qualifies as a cash flow hedge, to the extent that the hedge is effective, are recorded in other comprehensive income, until earnings are affected by the variability of cash flows of the hedged transaction (e.g., until periodic settlements of a variable-rate asset or liability are recorded in earnings). Any hedge ineffectiveness (which represents the amount by which the changes in the fair value of the derivative exceed the variability in the cash flows of the forecasted transaction) is recorded in current-period earnings.

Changes in the fair value of a derivative that is highly effective as and that is designated and qualifies as a foreign-currency hedge is recorded in either current-period earnings or other comprehensive income, depending on whether the hedging relationship satisfies the criteria for a fair value or cash flow hedge. If, however, a derivative is used as a hedge of a net investment in a foreign operation, the changes in the derivative's fair value, to the extent that the derivative is effective as a hedge, are recorded in the cumulative-translation-adjustment component of other comprehensive income. Changes in the fair value of derivative trading and nonhedging instruments are reported in current-period earnings.

The Company occasionally purchases a financial instrument in which a derivative instrument is "embedded." Upon purchasing the financial instrument, the Company assesses whether the economic characteristics of the embedded derivative are clearly and closely related to the economic characteristics of the remaining component of the financial instrument (i.e., the host contract) and whether a separate, nonembedded instrument with the same terms as the embedded instrument would meet the definition of a derivative instrument. When it is determined that (1) the embedded derivative possesses economic characteristics that are not clearly and closely related to the economic characteristics of the host contract and (2) a separate, stand-alone instrument with the same terms would qualify as a derivative instrument, the embedded derivative is separated from the host contract, carried at fair value, and designated as either (1) a fair value, cash flow, or foreign-currency hedge or (2) a trading or nonhedging derivative instrument. However, if the entire contract is measured at fair value, with changes in fair value reported in current earnings, or if the Company cannot reliably identify and measure the embedded derivative for purposes of separating that derivative from its host contract, the entire contract is carried on the balance sheet at fair value and is not designated as a hedging instrument.

The Company formally documents all relationships between hedging instruments and hedged items, as well as its risk-management objective and strategy for undertaking various hedge transactions. This process includes linking all derivatives that are designated as fair value, cash flow, or foreign-currency hedges to (1) specific assets and liabilities on the balance sheet or (2) specific firm commitments or forecasted transactions. The Company also formally assesses (both at the hedge's inception and on an ongoing basis) whether the derivatives that are used in hedging transactions have been highly effective in offsetting changes in the fair value or cash flows of hedged items and whether those derivatives may be expected to remain highly effective in future periods. When it is determined that a derivative is not (or has ceased to be) highly effective as a hedge, the Company discontinues hedge accounting prospectively, as discussed below.

The Company discontinues hedge accounting prospectively when (1) it determines that the derivative is no longer effective in offsetting changes in the fair value or cash flows of a hedged item (including hedged items such as firm commitments or forecasted transactions); (2) the derivative expires or is sold, terminated, or exercised; (3) it is no longer probable that the forecasted transaction will occur; (4) a hedged firm commitment no longer meets the definition of a firm commitment; or (5) management determines that designating the derivative as a hedging instrument is no longer appropriate or desired.

When hedge accounting is discontinued due to the Company's determination that the derivative no longer qualifies as an effective fair value hedge, the Company will continue to carry the derivative on the balance sheet at its fair value but cease to adjust the hedged asset or liability for changes in fair value. When hedge accounting is discontinued because the hedged item no longer meets the definition of a firm commitment, the Company will continue to carry the derivative on the balance sheet at its fair value, removing from the balance sheet any asset or liability that was recorded to recognize the firm commitment and recording it as a gain or loss in current-period earnings. When the Company discontinues hedge accounting because it is no longer probable that the forecasted transaction will occur in the originally expected period, the gain or loss on the derivative remains in accumulated other comprehensive income and is reclassified into earnings when the forecasted transaction affects earnings. However, if it is probable that a forecasted transaction will not occur by the end of the originally specified time period or within an additional two-month period of time thereafter, the gains and losses that were accumulated in other comprehensive income will be recognized immediately in earnings. In all situations in which hedge accounting is discontinued and the derivative remains outstanding, the Company will carry the derivative at its fair value on the balance sheet, recognizing changes in the fair value in current-period earnings.

2. Additional footnote disclosures for commercial/industrial users of fair value, cash flow, and net investment hedges

Fair Value Hedges

The Company enters into forward-exchange contracts to hedge the foreign-currency exposure of its firm commitments to purchase certain production parts from Germany and Brazil. The forward contracts that are used in this program mature in 18 months or less, consistent with the related purchase commitments. The Company generally hedges between 60 and 80 percent of its total firm-commitment purchase contracts.

The Company uses interest rate swaps to economically convert a portion of its nonprepayable fixed-rate debt into variable-rate debt. The resulting cost of funds is lower than it would have been if variable-rate debt had been issued directly. Under the interest rate swap contracts, the Company agrees with other parties to exchange, at specified intervals, the difference between fixed-rate and floating-rate interest amounts, which is calculated based on an agreed-upon notional amount. The level of variable-rate debt (after the effects of interest rate swaps have been considered) is maintained at 35 to 50 percent of the total Company debt.

The value of the Company's inventory of copper and aluminum raw materials changes daily, consistent with price movements in the respective commodities markets. The Company uses futures contracts to manage price risks associated with this inventory and generally hedges 70 to 75 percent of the inventory's total value.

For the year ended December 31, 20X0, the Company recognized a net gain of $XXX, (reported as [financial-statement line item caption] in the statement of operations), which represented the ineffective portion of all of the Company's fair value hedges. All components of each derivative's gain or loss were included in the assessment of hedge effectiveness. The Company also recognized a net gain of $XXX (reported as [financial statement line item caption] in the statement of operations) in relation to firm commitments that no longer qualified as fair value hedge items. The amounts discussed above are also referenced in Footnote X.

Cash Flow Hedges

The Company's direct-foreign-export sales are denominated in the customers' local currency. The Company purchases foreign-exchange put options and forward-exchange contracts as hedges of anticipated sales denominated in foreign currencies. The Company enters into these contracts to protect itself against the risk that the eventual dollar-net-cash inflows resulting from direct-foreign-export sales will be adversely affected by changes in exchange rates. Based on the Company's estimate of future foreign exchange rates, it hedges 50 to 75 percent of anticipated sales for the following 12 months.

The Company receives royalties from each of its European subsidiaries. The Company uses foreign-currency forward-exchange contracts and swap contracts that expire in less than 12 months to hedge against the effect that fluctuations in exchange rates may have on forecasted intercompany royalty cash flows. The Company purchases foreign-currency put options, with contract terms that normally expire within less than six months to hedge against the adverse effects that fluctuations in exchange rates may have on foreign-currency-denominated trade receivables.

The Company uses interest rate swaps to economically convert a portion of its variable-rate debt to fixed-rate debt. The resulting cost of funds is lower than it would have been had fixed-rate borrowings been issued directly. The level of fixed-rate debt, after the effects of interest rate swaps have been considered, is maintained at 50 to 65 percent of the total Company debt.

The Company enters into long-term sales contracts at spot prices with a number of its customers. As a hedge against possible price fluctuations in anticipated commodity purchases (which will be necessary to fulfill the sales contracts), the Company purchases copper and aluminum futures and options contracts. The futures and options contracts limit the unfavorable effect that potential price increases would have on metal purchases, and the futures contracts likewise limit the favorable effect of potential price declines.

For the year ended December 31, 20X0, the Company recognized a net loss of $XXX (reported as [financial-statement line item caption] in the statement of operations), which represented the total ineffectiveness of all cash flow hedges. All components of each derivative's gain or loss were included in the assessment of hedge effectiveness. In addition, after discontinuing certain of its cash flow hedges, the Company determined that it was not probable that certain forecasted transactions would occur by the end of the originally specified time period or within an additional two-month period of time thereafter. Therefore, the Company reclassified a net gain of $XXX as [financial-statement line item caption] into the statement of operations from accumulated other comprehensive income. The amounts discussed above are also referenced in Footnote X.

As of December 31, 20X0, $XXX of deferred net gains on derivative instruments accumulated in other comprehensive income are expected to be reclassified as earnings during the next 12 months. Transactions and events that: (1) are expected to occur over the next 12 months and (2) will necessitate reclassifying the derivative gains as earnings include (a) royalties earned, (b) actual direct-foreign-export sales, (c) the repricing of variable-rate debt, and (d) the sale of machinery and equipment that includes previously hedged purchases of aluminum and copper raw materials. The maximum term over which the Company is hedging exposures to the variability of cash flows (for all forecasted transactions, excluding interest payments on variable-rate debt) is 18 months. The amounts discussed above are also referenced in Footnote X.

Hedges of Net Investments in Foreign Operations

The Company has numerous investments in foreign subsidiaries. The net assets of these subsidiaries are exposed to volatility in currency exchange rates. The Company uses both derivative and nonderivative financial instruments to hedge this exposure and measures the ineffectiveness of such hedges based on the change in spot foreign exchange rates. The Company manages currency exposure related to the net assets of the Company's Latin American subsidiaries primarily through foreign-currency-denominated debt agreements that the Company (the "parent company") enters into. Gains and losses in the parent company's net investments in its subsidiaries are economically offset by losses and gains in the parent company's foreign-currency-denominated debt obligations.

The Company also enters into foreign-currency forward-exchange contracts to hedge the foreign-currency exposure of its investments in European and Asian subsidiaries. These agreements are in place for each subsidiary and have contract terms of nine months to one year.

For the year ended December 31, 20X0, $XXX of net losses related to (1) the foreign-currency-denominated debt agreements and (2) the forward exchange contracts were included in the Company's cumulative translation adjustment. For the same period, $XXX of net losses was recorded in earnings representing the amount of the hedges' ineffectiveness. The amounts discussed above are also referenced in Footnote X.

The presentation and disclosure requirements for derivative instruments and hedging activities are quite extensive. Companies that use derivatives to hedge their business risks must have extensive internal controls build around the documentation and the accounting for these financial instruments.

This book is designed to equip managers and executives with an understanding of the complex world of derivative instruments. The focus throughout the book is on operating managers and executives who are responsible for managing operating and financial risks that could adversely impact the company's financial position. My goal is to make the accounting for derivatives and hedging activities understandable. In addition, the goal of the book is have an accounting toolkit when evaluating the impacts on the financial statements when engaging in this type of risk management activities.

APPENDIX I

Scope Issues

About This Chapter

The accounting for derivatives model states that a derivative instrument is any contract that contains the following three elements.

1. The contract contains an underlying variable and a notional (principal) amount that if or when an event occurs causes variability of cash flows for one or both parties to the contract.
2. The contract has no initial net investment or an initial net investment that is smaller than other types of contracts and provides significant leveraging of returns.
3. The contract requires or permits net settlement; there are market mechanisms in place that would facilitate net settlement.

Because of this extremely broad definition of financial and nonfinancial contracts that would qualify as derivatives, accounting guidance allows for two types of exceptions: (1) Items that qualify as derivatives but are reported on financial statements using a different accounting guidance (guidance for a transaction is superseded by other accounting guidance) and (2) Derivatives that are scoped out of the accounting guidance for derivatives. This chapter will discuss the common exceptions to derivative accounting under each of the two categories above.

However, it is important to note that the derivative exceptions that are scoped out require careful documentation in meeting the exception requirements and the company **elects** not to account for them as derivatives.

Different Accounting Model

The contracts scoped out of the derivative accounting model include the following:

- equity contracts issued by the company,
- stock-based compensation awarded to employees,
- certain types of insurance contracts, and
- contracts issued that would be an impediment to sale accounting.

Equity Contracts Issued by the Company

Contracts that are issued or held by the company that are both (1) classified in stockholders equity and (2) indexed solely to their own stock are not to be accounted for under the derivative accounting model.[1] Move to appendix these contracts are exempted because accounting guidance states that derivatives are assets and liabilities. For example, when a company issues a call option on its own stock, the option may be exempted for derivative accounting if it represents an equity transaction. In making this determination, a company would use the following model.

1. *Evaluate any contingent provisions.* Contingency provisions are not based on (a) an observable market, other than the market for the company's own stock (if applicable) or an (b) observable index, other than those calculated or measured solely by the issuer's own operations.
2. Once the contingent event has occurred, the instruments amount is based solely on the issuer's stock
   a. Settlement amount must be equal to the fair value of a fixed number of equity shares and a fixed price or settlement amount. In other words, a fixed (shares) for fixed (cash or principal amount of a bond) comparison.

A word of caution, this is an extremely complex area of accounting. If your company has any of these transactions, you must consult the detailed accounting guidance and navigate carefully. A future book "Accounting for Capital Transactions: An Issuer's Perspective" will examine these difficult accounting transactions in-depth.

Share-Based Compensation

Accounting for stock or options issued to employees in return for services rendered as compensation is covered under other accounting guidance.[2]

However, when option contracts granted for employee service are modified, and the employee no longer is providing services to the company, the derivative accounting model then would be applied to the modification.

Normal Purchases and Normal Sales

Normal purchase and normal sales[3] are contracts that provide for the purchase or sale of something (inventory) other than a derivative financial instrument that will be delivered in quantities expected to be used or sold by the company over a reasonable period of time in the normal course of business. For example, the Company purchases forward contracts for physical delivery of 500,000 gallons of high fructose corn syrup for use in producing beverage products. The forward contracts are staggered to be delivered to the company at a rate of 100,000 gallons per month. In that case, since the commodity is used in the normal course of operations (producing beverages) and the time limit is reasonable, the forward contracts would meet the normal sales and purchases exception and the derivative instruments would not be accounting for as derivatives, but would instead be accounted for as and inventory purchase. The company delivering the high fructose corn syrup would likewise qualify for the normal sales exception and account for the forward contracts as sales when delivered.

The accounting guidance that provides an exception for normal business activities of having to apply the complex requirements of accounting for derivatives and hedging activities to inventory purchases or product sales provides a great deal of relief. However, since these are derivative instruments, the accounting guidance is very specific as to what would qualify for the normal sales and purchases exception from derivative accounting. In addition, the documentation for qualifying for this exception must be done at inception of each derivative contract.

To qualify for the scope exception, a contract's terms must be consistent with the terms of an entity's normal purchases or normal sales, that is, the quantity purchased or sold must be reasonable in relation to the entity's business needs. Determining whether or not the terms are consistent requires judgment.

In making those judgments, an entity should consider all relevant factors, including all of the following:

a. The quantities provided under the contract and the entity's need for the related assets

b. The locations to which delivery of the items will be made

c. The period of time between entering into the contract and delivery

d. The entity's prior practices with regard to such contracts.

Further, each of the following types of evidence should help in identifying contracts that qualify as normal purchases or normal sales:

a. Past trends

b. Expected future demand

c. Other contracts for delivery of similar items

d. An entity's and industry's customs for acquiring and storing the related commodities

e. An entity's operating locations. (endnote 815-10-15-15)

In addition to the accounting guidance above the underlying (forward rates on a forward contract to deliver a commodity) must be clearly and closely related to the asset being sold or purchased. This analysis is specific to the derivative contract being evaluated for the scope exception for normal sales and purchases. In other words, if the derivative contract contains a price adjustment for either party to the contract that is not a part of either the buyer's and seller's normal business practices for purchasing or selling commodities (which are sold and purchased at market prices) and is significant when compared to market transactions (fair value), then the exception test fails and we account for it as a derivative instrument.

For example, the clearly and closely related criteria for a forward contract that is a commodity would be a clause in the contract that would change the basis adjustment made for storage, transportation, or insurance. Since the basis adjustment would relate directly to the underlying commodity, the basis adjustment would be clearly and closely related to the physical commodity being delivered.

The documentation requirements for the normal purchases and normal sales scope exception may be applied to either (1) groups of contracts, or (2) an individual contract. In addition, the Board has stated that an entity may document which contracts are *not* designated as normal purchases and normal sales (i.e., when qualifying for the normal purchases and normal sales exceptions is normal for a company, it may be easier for that company to document contracts that do not qualify as normal purchases and normal sales). However, a company's documentation must be specific enough to enable a third party to determine which specific contracts are designated as normal purchases and normal sales. (endnote)

The other important scope exception for a derivative instrument is one that serves as an impediment to recording a sale (revenue) for the seller.[4] A derivative instrument whose existence serves as an impediment to recognizing a related contract as a sale by one party or a purchase by the counterparty is not subject to this accounting guidance for derivative instruments. For example, the existence of a guarantee of the residual value of a leased asset by the lessor may be an impediment to treating a contract as a sales type lease, in which case the contract would be treated by the lessor as an operating lease. Another example is the existence of a call option enabling a transferor to repurchase transferred assets that is an impediment to sales accounting. Such a call option on transferred financial assets that are not readily available would prevent accounting for that transfer as a sale. The consequence is that to recognize the call option would be to count the same thing twice. The holder of the option already recognizes in its financial statements the assets that it has the option to purchase. (endnote 815-10-15-63)

The following financial contracts that meet the definition of what constitutes a derivative are also scoped out of the accounting guidance or derivative instruments.

- Certain insurance contracts (life, health, property, casualty)
- Financial guarantee contracts
- Certain loan commitments
- Regular securities trades

This following may represent complex financial contracts that are to be carefully analyzed before a company can conclude that the scope exceptions apply for that particular contract.

APPENDIX II

Embedded Derivatives

If derivatives are embedded in a financial instrument or other contract, the base contract (i.e., excluding the embedded derivative) is referred to as the *host contract*. The combination of the host contract and the embedded derivative is referred to as the *hybrid instrument*. An example of a hybrid instrument is a structured note that pays interest based on changes in the S&P 500 Index; the component of the contract that is to adjust the interest payments based on changes in the S&P 500 Index is the embedded derivative, and the debt instrument component of the contract that is to pay interest without such adjustment and to repay the principal amount is the host contract.

Certain financial instruments and other contracts that do not in their entirety meet the definition of a derivative instrument (including prepayable loans, convertible bonds, insurance policies, and leases) often contain embedded derivative instruments with implicit or explicit terms that affect (1) some or all of the cash flows or (2) the value of other exchanges required by the contract in a manner similar to that of a derivative instrument. The effect of embedding a derivative instrument in a host contract is that some or all of the cash flows or other exchanges that otherwise would be required by the host contract (whether unconditional or contingent upon the occurrence of a specified event) will be modified based on an underlying (e.g., an interest rate, a price index, or some other index) that is applied to a notional amount (or there is a payment provision triggered by the underlying). It is that variability of the cash flows to be paid or received that is calculated based on the notional amount based on the movement of the underlying that requires the an analysis of whether the host contract contains an embedded derivative that needs to be bifurcated (separated) from the host contract.

Embedded derivatives can be difficult to identify because few host contracts will use the term derivative. Companies should be aware that embedding into contracts terms and conditions that vary the cash flows to be paid or received based on an underlying variable or the occurrence or nonoccurrence of and event may result in the identification of an embedded derivative.

After a company has identified that a derivative has been embedded in the contract, the next step is to determine if the derivative is an embedded derivative or a freestanding derivative[1]. If the derivative is determined to be freestanding, then it is required to be bifurcated (separated) from the host and accounted for as a derivative instrument apart from the host instrument. For example, the Company issues $10,000,000 of convertible debt at 5.25% with each 1,000 of debt convertible into 50 shares of the company's common stock at the holder's option. Under some circumstances, the put option held by the holder would be bifurcated by the issuer and the equity put option would be accounted for as a freestanding derivative instrument and the convertible debt would be accounting for as "straight" debt.

Therefore, although a derivative instrument may be written into the same contract as another instrument (i.e., in a debt agreement), it is considered embedded only if it cannot be legally separated from the host contract and transferred to a third party. If it cannot be separated from the host contract it would be scoped out of the accounting guidance for derivative instruments. In contrast, features that are written in the same contract, but that may be legally detached and separately exercised would be considered attached, freestanding derivatives rather than embedded derivatives by both the writer and the holder. These freestanding derivatives would be accounted for separately regardless of whether they meet the accounting guidance for bifurcation.

Prior to illustrating a common example of bifurcating an embedded derivative from the host contract, we will define a host contract and the criteria one uses in determining whether to account for an embedded derivative as a freestanding derivative instrument. A host contract is the contract that would have been issued if the hybrid instrument did not contain an embedded derivative (Issue straight debt instead of convertible debt). Each embedded derivative is compared to its host contract to determine if bifurcation of the hybrid instrument (i.e., into its host contract and embedded derivative components) would be required (accounted for as a freestanding derivative). Therefore, in order to apply the embedded derivative model, it is necessary to properly define the host contract based on its underlying economic characteristics and risks. This analysis is the key variable in determining whether the embedded derivative will be bifurcated from the host and accounting for as a freestanding derivative.

Accounting guidance states that an embedded derivative must be bifurcated from the host when "the economic characteristics and risks of the embedded derivative instrument are not clearly and closely related to the economic characteristics and risks of the host contract".[2] Said another way, if the host contract's change in price is due to a different market variable than the embedded derivative then accounting guidance states that the embedded derivative be bifurcated. For example, changes in value to debt are due to interest rate risk, changes in equity values are due to market or price risk.

To illustrate the financial statement impacts of one of the most common examples of how to account for an embedded derivative, we will illustrate the accounting for an equity-linked note. (endnote)

On January 1, 20X1, Company issues a two-year structured note with a principal amount of $1,000,000 indexed to the stock of an unrelated publicly traded entity (A Company). At maturity, the holder of the instrument will receive the principal amount plus any appreciation or minus any depreciation in the fair value of 10,000 shares of A Company, with changes in fair value measured from the issuance date of the debt instrument. The note bears a floating rate of interest. The market price of A Company shares is as follows: $100 per share at the issuance date; $90 at December 31, 20X1, and $125 on December 31, 20X2.

Identifying the Embedded Derivative

The host contract is a debt instrument because the instrument has a stated maturity and because the holder has none of the rights of a shareholder, such as the ability to vote the shares and receive distributions to shareholders. *The embedded derivative is an equity-based forward contract (it provides upside and downside potential) that has as its underlying the fair value of the stock of Alta Properties.* The forward-based derivative should initially be recorded at its fair value of $0. That is, all of the proceeds should be ascribed to the debt host contract. (endnote ASC 815-15-30-4 and-30-5) Subsequently, the debt host is accounted for as debt by Company and as a debt security by the investors. The forward contract should be marked to market through earnings as a freestanding derivative.

> **Note:** The journal entries below treat the forward contract as a separate asset or liability to emphasize that the embedded derivative and host contract are measured separately. For financial reporting purposes, companies should combine the fair value of the derivative with the carrying amount of the host contract. For this illustration, we will record the financial statement effects for the issuer of the structured note.

Issuer's Accounting (Company)

Financial Statement Template

Assets =	Liabilities +	Stockholder's Equity
		+ Gain on forward contract – Loss on forward contract

Company would record the following journal entries (for brevity, the accrual of interest is not presented below):

January 1, X1
To record the issuance of the structured note as debt:

+ Cash + 1,000,000	+ Debt + Debt 1,000,000	

Assets =	Liabilities +	Stockholder's Equity
+ Cash + 1,000,000		

Assets =	Liabilities +	Stockholder's Equity
	+ Debt + 1,000,000	

Note: at inception, the entire proceeds are recorded at the amount of the proceeds received for the issuance of the structured note. Since the forward contract at inception has zero value all of the proceeds are recorded as debt.

December 31, X1

To record the change in fair value of the forward contract [(90 − 100) × −$10,000]:

+Forward contract +100,000		+Gain on forward contract +100,000

Assets =	Liabilities +	Stockholder's Equity
+ Forward contract + 100,000		

Assets =	Liabilities +	Stockholder's Equity
		+ Gain on forward contract + 100,000

Note: The computation of the forward contract fair value change is computed as demonstrated above. The logic is if we paid off the debt as of this date we would write off the debt at $1,000,000 and write off the asset account forward contract at $100,000 and the remainder would be a decrease in cash of $900,000. The gain on forward reduces the amount of cash to be paid if we had paid off the debt.

December 31, 20X2

To record the change in fair value of the fair value of the forward contract [(125−90) × − $10,000]:

Assets =	Liabilities +	Stockholder's Equity
	+ Forward contract liability + 350,000	

Assets =	Liabilities +	Stockholder's Equity
		− Loss of forward contract − 350,000

Note: the fair value change of ($90 − $125) × 10,000 =$350,000 has changed the asset account to a liability account with a balance of $250,000.

To record settlement of the debt contract with investors:

Assets =	Liabilities +	Stockholder's Equity
– Cash – 1,250,000	.	

Assets =	Liabilities +	Stockholder's Equity
	– Forward contract liability – 250,000 – Debt – 1,000,000	

Note: the forward contract liability of $250,000 that is written off will increase the amount of cash to be paid to settle the debt to $1,250,000.

The accounting for embedded derivatives, similar to accounting for derivative instruments in general, can be very complex. The intricacies involved in even recognizing an embedded derivative and then performing the analysis of whether the embedded derivatives should be accounted for as freestanding derivatives will depend on the terms and conditions of the contract. A detailed discussion of the many instances of embedded derivatives is beyond the scope of this book. However, that being said, any clause embedded in a contract that could cause the amount paid or received to vary and the amount is based on the underlying variable interacting with the notional (principal) amount owed or received is potentially an embedded derivative that would cause a company analysis to determine if the derivative is freestanding and requires bifurcation from the host.

Notes

Chapter 1

1. Financial Accounting Standards Board (FASB), Accounting Standards Codification (ASC), 815-10-15-83
2. Adapted for Ernst and Young. (2012). Financial Reporting Developments: *Derivative Instruments and Hedging Activities*, from www.ey.com.us/ accounting link
3. FASB ASC 815-20-20 Glossary
4. FASB 815-20-20 Glossary
5. Adapted from PWC National Professional Service Group. (2012). *Guide to Accounting for Derivative Instruments and Hedging Activities* from www. cfodirect.com/guides
6. FASB ASC 820—Fair Value Measurements
7. Adapted from FASB ASC 815-10-55

Chapter 2

1. FASB ASC 815-20-25-80
2. PWC (2012)
3. FASB ASC 815-20-25-3
4. FASB ASC 815-20-25-3(d)
5. FASB ASC 815-20-25-28
6. FASB ASC 815-20-25-31
7. FASB ASC 815-20-25-75 through 81
8. PWC (2012)
9. FASB ASC 815-20-25-102 through 111 and FASB ASC 815-20-55-71
10. FASB ASC 815-20-35-2 through 4

Chapter 3

1. All problems are adapted from FASB ASC 815-25-55 and from PWC (2012) and E&Y (2011)

Chapter 4

1. All problems are adapted from FASB ASC 815-25-55 and from PWC (2012) and E&Y (2011)

Chapter 5

1. All problems are adapted from FASB ASC 815-25-55 and from PWC (2012) and E&Y (2011)

Chapter 6

1. FASB ASC 815-10-50-1 through 4(d)
2. FASB ASC 815-20-25-58 through 66
3. FASB ASC 815-20-50-1 through 5
4. E&Y (2011)

Appendix I

1. FASB ASC 480 and FASB ASC 815-10-15-74(a)
2. FASB ASC 480 and FASB ASC 815-10-15-74(b)
3. FASB 815-25-50-1 through 5
4. E&Y (2011)

Appendix II

1. FASB ASC 815-15-25-1
2. FASB ASC 815-15-25-1

Index

OTHER TITLES IN OUR FINANCE AND FINANCIAL MANAGEMENT COLLECTION

- *An Executive's Guide for Moving from US GAAP to IFRS* by Peter Walton
- *Effective Financial Management: The Cornerstone for Success* by Geoff Turner
- *Financial Reporting Standards: A Decision-Making Perspective for Non-Accountants* by David Doran
- *Revenue Recognition: Principles and Practices* by Frank Beil
- *Accounting for Derivatives and Hedging Activities* by Frank Beil

ALSO IN FORTHCOMING IN THIS COLLECTION

- *Accounting Fraud Maneuvering and Manipulation, Past and Present* by Gary Giroux 12/31/2013
- *Accounting for Business Combinations* by Frank J Beil 1/15/2014
- *Accounting for Capital Transactions: An Issuer's Perspective* by Frank J. Beil 5/15/2014
- *The Use of Fair Value Measurements in Accounting* by Frank J. Beil 7/15/2014
- *Using Financial Statements: Analyzing, Forecasting, Decision-Making 8/15/2015*
- *International Auditing Standards in the United States: Comparing and Understanding Standards for ISA and PCAOB* by Asokan Anandarajan and Gary Kleinman 11/15/2014

Announcing the Business Expert Press Digital Library

Concise E-books Business Students
Need for Classroom and Research

This book can also be purchased in an e-book collection by your library as
- a one-time purchase,
- that is owned forever,
- allows for simultaneous readers,
- has no restrictions on printing, and
- can be downloaded as PDFs from within the library community.

Our digital library collections are a great solution to beat the rising cost of textbooks. e-books can be loaded into their course management systems or onto student's e-book readers.

The **Business Expert Press** digital libraries are very affordable, with no obligation to buy in future years. For more information, please visit **www.businessexpertpress.com/librarians**. To set up a trial in the United States, please contact **Adam Chesler** at *adam.chesler@businessexpertpress.com* for all other regions, contact **Nicole Lee** at *nicole.lee@igroupnet.com*.

CPSIA information can be obtained at www.ICGtesting.com
Printed in the USA
BVOW11s0601290114

343202BV00003B/7/P